Praise for

The Seven Questions You're Asked in Heaven

"I really love this book! Ron Wolfson teaches us to focus on what is ultimately important in life through a close analysis of some religious sources and a plethora of stories that make his points compelling and real. I laughed in some parts of this book and cried in others, but throughout I felt that I had a great friend who was teaching me to live my life according to what counts. A pleasure to read and a blessing at the same time."

—**Rabbi Elliot N. Dorff, PhD,** author,
The Way Into Tikkun Olam (Repairing the World)

"In his highly inviting and readable style, Ron Wolfson provides us with a map for life's journey—an indispensable spiritual GPS for the twenty-first century."

—**Sandy Eisenberg Sasso,** author of many children's books
including, *God's Paintbrush* and a book for adults,
God's Echo: Exploring Scripture with Midrash

"With his accessible, signature style, Dr. Wolfson weaves an easy tapestry of Jewish life-wisdom. He effortlessly integrates sources from the Bible to the *New York Times*, from the Hasidic masters to personal vignettes from his own life experience. Gives us the perfect preparation workbook for a spiritual life."

—**Rabbi Lawrence Kushner,** Emanu-El Scholar, Congregation
Emanu-El of San Francisco; author, *Invisible Lines of Connection:
Sacred Stories of the Ordinary,* and many other books

"Wakes us up to the reality that it is much more important to ask what happens if we dare to live. Last Rosh Hashanah, I challenged my students to become angels by reading *God's To-Do List*. This year we will strive to become truly human by working on our answers to the Seven Questions."

—**Rabbi David Levy,** university chaplain, Colgate University

"With wit, charm and personal stories gleaned from his and others' life-experiences, Wolfson has made accessible all the wisdom and theology of the Bible and rabbinic writings with regard to living a meaningful life. A must read for those searching for a means to reshape and reprioritize their lives to find greater meaning and purpose—bringing heaven to earth."

—**Rabbi Steven Wernick,** executive vice president and CEO, The United Synagogue of Conservative Judaism

"A beautiful guide to living a meaningful life. Serves as a much-needed reminder that we will be remembered not for our material success, but for our relationships, our contribution to creating a better world, and our care for the well-being of others."

—**Rabbi Jill Jacobs,** Rabbi-in-Residence, Jewish Funds for Justice; author, *There Shall Be No Needy: Pursuing Social Justice through Jewish Law and Tradition*

"Walks us through the most important questions that can shape meaningful, authentic, joyous living. Draws us forward in search of our own answers, handing us the tools we need as we advance."

—**Rabbi Bradley Shavit Artson,** dean, Ziegler School of Rabbinic Studies; vice president, American Jewish University

"God has questions. Ron Wolfson shows us the answers. With warmth, humor, and wisdom, he shares the secrets of a life of purpose and meaning. This is a book to be read carefully, to be learned, to be cherished."

—**Rabbi Edward Feinstein,** rabbi, Valley Beth Shalom; author, *Tough Questions Jews Ask: A Young Adult's Guide to Building a Jewish Life*

"With wisdom, warmth, and humor, Ron Wolfson leads us to the gates of the World to Come. Focuses our attention on what really matters in living. As a trustworthy, learned friend, Wolfson offers reflection, inspiration, and direction on life's most important questions."

—**Rabbi Elie Kaplan Spitz,** author, *Healing from Despair: Choosing Wholeness in a Broken World*

The Seven Questions You're Asked in Heaven

REVIEWING & RENEWING YOUR LIFE ON EARTH

DR. RON WOLFSON

author of *God's To-Do List:*

103 Ways to Be an Angel and Do God's Work on Earth

For People of All Faiths, All Backgrounds

JEWISH LIGHTS Publishing

Woodstock, Vermont

The Seven Questions You're Asked in Heaven:
Reviewing and Renewing Your Life on Earth

2009 Quality Paperback Edition, First Printing
© 2009 by Ron Wolfson

For information regarding permission to reprint material from this book, please write or fax your request to Jewish Lights Publishing, Permissions Department, at the address / fax number listed below, or e-mail your request to permissions@jewishlights.com.

Library of Congress Cataloging-in-Publication Data
Wolfson, Ron.
The seven questions you're asked in heaven : reviewing and renewing your life on earth / Ron Wolfson.
p. cm.
Includes bibliographical references.
ISBN-13: 978-1-58023-407-8 (quality pbk.)
ISBN-10: 1-58023-407-0 (quality pbk.)
1. Spiritual life—Judaism. 2. Self-actualization (Psychology)—Religious aspects—Judaism. 3. Jewish way of life. I. Title.
BM723.W654 2009
296.7—dc22

2009017101

Manufactured in the United States of America
Cover Design: Jenny Buono

For People of All Faiths, All Backgrounds
Published by Jewish Lights Publishing
A Division of LongHill Partners, Inc.
Sunset Farm Offices, Route 4, P.O. Box 237
Woodstock, VT 05091
Tel: (802) 457-4000   Fax: (802) 457-4004
www.jewishlights.com

For my descendants
From your ancestor

∞ CONTENTS

THE ULTIMATE QUESTION

When you get to heaven, you'll be asked Seven Questions.
They aren't like the questions you've been asked in a job interview or to get into college. You won't be asked about your strengths or your weaknesses.

You won't be asked about your skills or your hobbies.

These are different questions. Transformative questions.

The Seven Questions you're asked in heaven are designed for one purpose, and one purpose only.

Here's the purpose:

You'll be asked Seven Questions in heaven that reveal how you lived your life on earth.

You will be asked questions that go to the very heart of a life that matters.

Because you get to know them now, you can use the questions to shape a life of purpose and meaning, a life well lived.

You see, embedded in the questions are answers—answers to the ultimate question:

Is the life you've lived here on earth worthy of a place in heaven?

If you can hear the questions and apply them to the way you live your life today, then when the time comes, your soul will be ready to take that stairway to heaven, prepared to answer the Seven Questions with a resounding "Yes!," and take your rightful place among the angels.

"Heaven, I'm in Heaven"

"Okay, Ron, I'm curious. But, how do you know (a) there is a *heaven*, and (b) someone will be there asking me questions?!"

As a person of faith, I believe there is a heaven. For me, it is a place where my soul goes after it leaves my human body. I am not sure what heaven looks like or even where it is. I am not even sure who asks the Seven Questions. Is it God? The angels? A heavenly attorney?

It doesn't really matter to me. What matters is this:

For thousands and thousands of years, human beings have imagined heaven—a place, a "state of being," some "next step"—where souls go after death. Virtually every religion has such a concept. Some have created quite detailed descriptions of what heaven might be like. Since no one has come back to give an accurate account, all we can do is imagine.

More interesting than what heaven looks like are the various scenarios developed by religious leaders, philosophers, and thinkers detailing how you "get in" to heaven and what happens once you enter. What qualifies you for admission? Does someone greet you at the door?

For Christians, admission depends on a belief that Jesus died to absolve you of your sins. For Muslims, repenting and good deeds pave the way. For Jews, how you live your life in this world determines your status in the *olam ha-bah,* literally, "the world to come."

Whatever your religion, according to a survey conducted by the Pew Forum on Religion and Public Life in August 2008, 65 percent of Americans said they believed that religions other than theirs could lead to "eternal life." So what gets you "in" to heaven? In the Pew study, 29 percent assert that actions are most important, 30 percent say belief is the key factor, and 10 percent hold that a combination of good deeds and belief is the best path. Only 7 percent of Americans do not believe in an afterlife. The results reveal a deep hope that good things will eventually come to good people.

Even Hollywood has ventured ideas about what happens when you get to heaven. Popular movies such as *Heaven Can Wait* and *Down to Earth,* both based on Harry Segall's *Here Comes Mr. Jordan,* imagine an interplay between heaven and earth. The classic film *It's a Wonderful Life* depicts a heaven where guardian angels watch over individual human beings;

Clarence, an angel-in-training, must help George Bailey see how he made a difference in the world and thus "earn his wings."

Defending Your Life

In his film *Defending Your Life,* Albert Brooks dramatizes the idea that we are asked questions about how we lived this life when we get to the next. After a sudden and fatal accident, his character, Daniel, finds himself in Judgment City, where he undergoes a type of trial, complete with lawyers, evidence, and, of course, judges. Specific incidents in his life are examined, cross-examined, and analyzed, all for the purpose of determining whether Daniel can "move forward" to the next stage of the afterlife. Apparently, Judgment City is not exactly heaven, but you do get to eat as much gourmet food as you want without gaining weight! In the end, the questioning encourages Daniel to look critically at his life on earth, confront a character flaw, and demonstrate his ability to learn and grow.

In the Jewish tradition, the Rabbis of the Talmud envision a Heavenly Court that reviews the lifetime of a person upon arrival in the next world. The imagery includes a "scale" to weigh the accumulated "good deeds" on the one hand and "sins" (where we "miss the mark") on the other. The ultimate Judge, God, considers the case and renders judgment. This mirrors the yearly "accounting of the soul" (*cheshbon ha-nefesh*), the spiritual goal of the Jewish High Holy Day period between Rosh Hashanah, the New Year, and Yom Kippur, the Day of Atonement.

"Knockin' on Heaven's Door"

The poet and musician Bob Dylan wrote a powerful song about the moment of meeting death. Dylan imagined he would be "knock, knock, knockin' on heaven's door."

And, when the door opens, what will you find? Who will you find? What are you asked? How will you answer?

I will tell you upfront the secret insight of this book:

It's not about the answers.

The answers will be different for each of us.

It's all about the questions.

The right questions.

The questions that get to the heart of a life well lived.

The Seven Questions you're asked in heaven can help you shape the answers that are your life's journey.

Five Plus One Plus One

What do you think you'll be asked when you get to heaven?

Really.

Stop a moment and consider this question about questions.

If you wish, write down here whatever immediately comes to mind:

_____

_____

_____

_____

Over the years, I've posed this question to many people—friends, colleagues, even some famous personalities, authors, artists, and teachers. You will find some of these "heavenly questions" along with other inspiring quotes displayed in boxes throughout the book. Here are some of the questions they expect:

Were you a good person?

Were you successful?

Were you popular?

Were you a good parent, spouse, sibling, daughter, or son?

Did you make a lot of money?

Did you make a contribution to society?

Did you take care of your family?

Did you give to charity?

Were you famous?

Were you good at your job?

Were you a believer?

Why do you deserve to be here?

Whom do you wish you could bring with you?

Whom do you want to reassure that you are in a good place?

What are the biggest insights of your life?

Whom would you want to have with you here in heaven?

Did you use your time well?

Did you eat too much? Drink too much?

Did you wear the latest fashions?

Did you exercise?

Did you answer all your e-mails?

I asked an irreverent good friend what he thought he would be asked when he got to heaven. He did not hesitate:

"What the *hell* are *you* doing here?"

All interesting questions, to be sure. But I went back to the sources I love from the Jewish tradition to look for what the Rabbis thought the questions in heaven might be.

And I found seven.

Five from one Rabbi.

One from another.

And one final question from a third.

Seven Questions you're asked in heaven.

Frankly, they are surprising. Unexpected. Not at all what I thought I would find. Nothing like the questions I've collected over the years.

I think you'll find them surprising, too.

Who's Asking?

Permit me to introduce to you the Jewish teachers who pose the Seven Questions you're asked in heaven.

Rabbi Abba ben Joseph bar Hama, known simply as Rava, was an important and influential authority among the group of Babylonian scholars whose debates over Jewish law fill the pages of the Talmud. In all but six instances, Rava's decisions were deemed the accepted legal practice—*halachah*. A popular teacher in his time (we are unsure of when he was born, but he died in 352 CE), Rava established an academy of scholars in the town of Machoza, became a wealthy landowner and vintner, and was a respected intermediary with the Persian authorities. In short, he was a man of the people as well as a teacher of Torah. In the Babylonian Talmud (Shabbat 31a), Rava imagines six questions you're asked in heaven. I have combined two similar queries into one, resulting in the first five of our Seven Questions.

Rabbi Samson Raphael Hirsch (1805–1888) was the intellectual founder of a popular contemporary Orthodox Judaism in nineteenth-century Germany. He wrote notable commentaries on the Pentateuch, Psalms, and the Jewish prayer book, as well as ethical and philosophical works. The story of his deathbed request is the basis of our Sixth Question.

Meshulam Zusya of Hanipoli (died in 1800), known simply as Zusya, was an early leader of Hasidism, an ecstatic expression of Judaism popularized in Eastern Europe in the eighteenth century. Zusya gained fame as stories of his wanderings spread among the early Kabbalists. Known as a modest man, unlike most great scholars of his time, Zusya nevertheless gathered disciples in Hanipoli, and folktales attest to his humble piety and simple wisdom. His concern about what he would be asked in heaven, told in an oft-cited story, gives us our final Question.

To be sure, there are many other Rabbis through the ages who have imagined what questions would be asked during a life review. Consider this prediction from the Talmud, written within the same historical period as Rava lived:

> When a person departs to the eternal home, all of his deeds are enumerated and he is told: "Such and such a thing have you done, in such and such a place on that day." The person then responds: "You have judged me correctly."
>
> Taanit 11a

In the Zohar, the central text of Kabbalah mysticism, Rabbi Eliezer is quoted as saying:

> On the day when a person's time arrives to depart from the world … three messengers stand over him and take an account of his life

and all that he has done in this world, and he admits with all of his mouth and signs the account with his hand ... so that he should be judged in the next world for all his actions, former and later, old and new, not one of them is forgotten.

Zohar I, 79a

This is the ultimate accounting of the soul—*cheshbon ha-nefesh*—the tallying up of the good and not-so-good things we do in a lifetime on earth. Notice that this accounting is done individually for each and every person. In short, the Rabbis are saying that each of us is "soul-ly" accountable for our actions.

By *each and every individual,* Judaism *means* each and every individual, Jew and non-Jew, who believes in one God. In Judaism, unlike other faith traditions, every human being—Jewish or not—qualifies for review. Although debated in the Talmud, this rather amazing universalistic notion is documented in Maimonides' Code of Jewish Law: "The pious of the nations of the world have a portion in the world to come" (Laws of Repentance 3:5). This reminds me of an old advertising tagline in New York City for a particular brand of rye bread. Above a series of photos of all sorts of people representing different ethnicities and races, the tagline reads: "You don't have to be Jewish to love Levy's."

You don't have to be Jewish to get into heaven.

But you will be asked questions.

Seven Questions.

1

To Tell the Truth

I enjoy David Letterman's late-night television show. He can be acerbic, true, but I find him very funny. A highlight of his program virtually every night is his "Top Ten List" about a topic of current interest. He always begins with Number Ten and counts down to the Number One question or statement, usually the funniest of the punch lines.

Number One is the most important.

So, what do you think the Number One Question you're asked in heaven will be?

The Number One.

The opening query.

The most important one.

Our teacher, Rava, begins our journey through the Seven Questions:

> At the hour you enter [heaven] for judgment, they will ask you ...
> *Nasata v'natata b'emunah?*
> Did you deal honestly with people in your business practices?
>
> Shabbat 31a

What?!?!

Are you kidding me?!?!

The *first* thing I'm asked is: "Were you an honest businessperson?"

Not "Do you believe in God?"

Not "Did you follow the Ten Commandments?"

Not "Did you give to charity?"

Not "Did you become famous?"

Whoa!

Let's think about this for a moment.

And ask a question about the Number One Question.

Why on earth—or, rather, why in heaven's name—would the first question be about business?

Look carefully at the text.

It's not just about business.

It's about honesty, integrity, faithfulness.

If you are not honest in your business dealings, can you be trusted to be honest in other relationships?

If you are not honest with others, can you be honest with yourself?

If you are not faithful with others, can your faith in God be trusted?

God knows, it's very tempting to fudge a little on the truth, to tell a little white lie.

God knows.

That's exactly the point Rava is driving home.

> **It's not easy to live with lies.**

You might believe that God is omnipresent, that God sees everything, that God knows everything.

Or you might believe the powerful metaphor of the Jewish High Holy Days: God, the Supreme Judge and Accountant, keeps books detailing personal deeds, good and bad, a kind of cosmic Santa Claus who knows who's been naughty or nice.

Or you may not.

But would you be willing to concede that, as much as you would like to hide your "unfaithful" business dealings from others, you can't hide them from *yourself*?

It's not easy to live with lies.

Honest to God.

Thrown for a Loupe

Is there any major purchase that inspires greater concern than buying jewelry? Most people have no idea what to look for in a diamond, pearl, or other precious gem. So they must trust the jeweler that the stones are what he or she says they are. There are even cases of dishonest jewelers passing off cubic zirconium as real diamonds. Only a well-schooled consumer can tell the difference between what is fake and what is real.

Antoinette Matlins is one of the world's foremost authorities on fine gems and jewelry. Author of half a dozen reference books and buying guides, she offers lectures and workshops around the world, teaching consumers and people in the gem trade how to assess the true value of a precious stone. Antoinette tells the following horror story:

So often we think we are clever and sophisticated and know the "right people" to take care of our every need. And so it is with those who love gems and jewelry and are able to acquire whatever their hearts desire. But I have come to realize that just as the factors affecting the rarity, quality, and value of any gem are not readily seen with the naked eye, so it is with people.

While lecturing about gems and jewelry aboard one of the world's premier cruise ships—providing information to help passengers avoid rip-offs ashore—I decided to give a workshop to teach passengers how to use a jeweler's loupe (pronounced loop), a small eye magnifier. This small tool is indispensable to professionals, enabling them to see microscopic features that help tell them what a stone really is, and to evaluate its rarity, quality, and value.

One of my "students" in the workshop was a tall, elegant, and very wealthy man who showed nothing but arrogance toward me. He made it clear to me—and to everyone else—that he did not need my expertise or that of anyone else; he was smart, sophisticated, and well traveled—and, he knew how to negotiate deals. Moreover, he had visited the port we were approaching many times and had been buying diamonds from a trusted dealer there for years. Imagine my surprise when he asked me to borrow a loupe to take ashore with him. I was delighted, reviewed briefly what he should do, and he confidently set off to his favored store in order to find five diamonds of "the highest quality" to set into a ring for his wife.

When he entered the store, he kept the loupe in his pocket. He explained what he wanted—five round brilliant-cut diamonds, about one-quarter carat each, of the very finest quality—and waited while the store owner put together a selection of stones for his consideration. The tray of diamonds was set before him. "These are my very best stones," the dealer assured him. It was only at this point—after a selection of the best-quality stones were sitting before him—that my student removed the loupe from his pocket. He picked up one of the diamonds and brought both the diamond and the loupe to his eye as I had taught him to do. But before he could even begin to examine it, the dealer swooped up the tray and said: "Oh, my! I just realized I picked up the wrong tray! These are the wrong stones!"

By the time the dealer realized his mistake of attempting to dupe "just another rich tourist," my student was walking out the door, devastated that he had been hoodwinked all these years. When he returned to the ship, he told me that the same thing happened in store after store: As soon as the loupe appeared, so did better stones! "You know, Antoinette," he admitted, "the loupe helped me see things more clearly—and I'm not referring just to the diamonds! I'm not sure what I was seeing in the stones, but it sure gave me the ability to see the flaws in the dealer!"

Kosher?

My wife, Susie, and I were newlyweds, living in a Midwest city where both of us were going to college. *Young* newlyweds. I was four months away from turning twenty-one; Susie had just turned twenty … and she looked like she was fourteen. We had decided to keep a kosher home and sought out a butcher shop to patronize. One day, we walked into a prominent purveyor of kosher meat and products in town and, much to our surprise, there were no prices indicated on the cuts of meat displayed in the case. The long, narrow trays had beautiful layers of chops and steaks with small signs—"Chuck Roast," "Rib Eye," and so on.

It was our first visit to the store and the owners did not know us.

"What can I get for you?" one of the two owners asked.

"How much is the ground beef per pound?" I replied.

Instead of answering directly, the first owner turned to the second and said in Yiddish, "Who are they?"

"I don't know," the second owner answered.

"What shall we charge them?"

"$3.95," the second said.

All of a sudden, Susie turned to me and said, "Ronnie, let's get out of here."

I had no idea what had just happened. When we got to our car, Susie explained. She knew the going price for kosher ground beef was about $2 a pound; they were overcharging us.

What the owners didn't know was that Susie had grown up in a home where Yiddish was the first language. In fact, Yiddish *was* Susie's native language.

Instead of being cheated, we felt devastated. If our commitment to keeping kosher had not been so strong, the incident may very well have turned us off to the idea entirely. Needless to say, we never shopped there again.

Thirty-eight years later, the largest processor of kosher meat in the United States is under investigation for allegedly questionable hiring of underage immigrant workers and other unethical practices. In response to this and other apparent lapses of honesty in the kosher food industry, the Conservative movement has proposed a set of ethical kashrut guidelines to ensure that both workers and animals have been properly and humanely treated in such facilities. The *Hechsher Tzedek* (literally, "righteous kashrut certificate") initiative seeks to add a layer of social justice to the ritual requirement. As Rabbi Morris Allen, the founder of the effort, says: "*Hechsher Tzedek* is a holistic celebration of Jewish tradition, uniting ethical practice with ritual observance in the production of Jewish food. Jewish law is concerned not only about the smoothness of a cow's lung, but also about the safety of a worker's hand as well as the impact that kosher food production has on the environment. *Hechsher Tzedek* grows out of Jewish tradition; it does not seek to redefine kashrut as much as enhance it."

Made Off

As I write these words, the entire world is reeling from the fallout of the largest Ponzi scheme in history, an illegal scam that worked because unwitting investors believed in the honesty of the perpetrator. Bernard Madoff, a well-known Wall Street investor and money manager, pled guilty to being the mastermind of a private investment fund that paid old investors with money from new investors, rather than with actual earned profits. Considered a philanthropist and an upstanding citizen by the many people and institutions that entrusted him with their funds, Madoff lost more than $64 billion of other people's money, wiping out entire charitable foundations and the accumulated wealth of untold numbers of investors. It may take years to sort out what actually happened and how he did it, but the bottom line is that Madoff betrayed their trust. His dishonesty brought financial ruin to friends, family, and communal institutions, and his misdeeds will have ripple effects and repercussions for years to come.

> The cost of dishonesty is incalculable.

Madoff committed another offense: He brought shame upon the Jewish people. Many of the charities and nonprofit organizations that lost hundreds of millions of dollars served the Jewish community. Madoff was not only dishonest, but he also stole vast sums of money, deceived people who trusted him, and made a mockery of the notion that all Jews are "sureties" for one another: *Kol Yisrael aveirim zeh ba-zeh*. According to Rabbi Burton L. Visotzky, a professor at The Jewish Theological Seminary of America, this means that "if a Jew takes a loan out, in some ways the whole Jewish community guarantees it." This sense of close communal ties—looking out for one another—led many Jewish institutions and individuals to seek out an opportunity to invest with someone they thought was honest. Sadly, it appears that Bernard Madoff was anything but honest in his business dealings. Lives were ruined, institutions were decimated, and an entire people was humiliated and embarrassed. And the perpetrator, once lauded as a great philanthropist and upstanding businessman, will forever be seen as a pariah.

The cost of dishonesty is incalculable.

Scales

The Lord demands accurate scales and balances; God sets the standards for fairness.

Proverbs 16:11

One day, I was waiting in line at a deli in our local supermarket. A woman in front of me was shopping for cheese. "I'll take a pound of cheddar," she gruffly instructed the clerk. In short order, the clerk placed a huge block of cheese in a slicer, which whirred into action. Layering the slices on a scale, the digital readout slowly climbed toward 1.00. But just as the clerk put down the last slice of cheese, her hand rested ever so slightly on the scale. "Take your thumb off there!" the shopper screamed. Horrified, the clerk quickly put both arms in the air as if she were in a holdup. "Look," the clerk cried, "no hands!" Clearly the shopper had been cheated in the past by heavy-thumbed deli clerks. Yet I was shocked by the distrust in this simple business transaction.

Have you ever noticed that scales are regularly inspected to ensure accuracy? You can find little seals of approval from government officials who have tested the weight scales at deli counters and the gas pumps at what used to be called "service stations."

We want our scales to be honest. We want to trust their measurements.

Balance

Take out a dollar bill from your purse or wallet.

Look at the green seal of the Department of Treasury on the right side of the front of the bill; it appears under the superimposed word *ONE*.

On the shield inside the logo, do you see the scales?

There are two pans, suspended from the top arm of the scale, perfectly balanced. They are meant to represent the scales used by assayers in the nineteenth century. You've seen them used in old Westerns depicting the gold rush. Assayers would put the gold nuggets brought to them by prospectors on one pan, using weights placed on the other pan to weigh the ore.

> Did I live a
> balanced life?
> _____
> JUDY BIN-NUN

Think of the "scales of justice," an image often used by courts and law firms. Lady Justice holds the scales; she is blind-folded—justice is blind. The pans in this scale represent innocence on one side, guilt on the other. A jury listens to the case and then "weighs the evidence" in order to reach a verdict.

It's all about balance.

Balancing the pans.

Balancing the scales.

I asked a friend what she thought she would be asked when she got to heaven. She thought for a few seconds and said: "Did I live a balanced life? Was I able to strike a balance between work and rest? Was I able to balance my career and my family?"

Are you leading a life in balance?

Accounting

Scales and ledgers and balance sheets are really all about one thing: measurement.

The hit song "Seasons of Love" from the musical *Rent* asks the question "How do you measure the life of a woman or man?" How *do* you measure a year? Is it just five hundred twenty-five thousand six hundred minutes? Are there other ways to measure a year or a life? Jonathan Larsen, the late creator of *Rent* answers: "How about love?"

"Measuring" is about accountability. How can you be accountable in heaven if you're not accountable on earth?

The Seven Questions are designed to reveal how you measure up.

If the scales and ledgers and balance sheets are not accurate, your measurement will be off.

Complete and Honest

In the Bible, the Israelites are told of the importance of honest weights and measures:

> You shall not have in your pouch alternate weights, larger and smaller. You shall not have in your house alternate measures, a larger and a smaller. You must have complete and honest weights and complete and honest measures, if you are to endure long on the soil that the Lord your God is giving you. For everyone who does those things, everyone who deals dishonestly, is abhorrent to the Lord your God.

> Deuteronomy 25:13–16

Notice that *using* dishonest weights is not the only thing prohibited here; you cannot *own* them. This principle formed the basis of a stable and just economic society. Notice also that you cannot have dishonest weights in your "pouch"—that is, your business; nor may you have them in your "house"—your home.

In this text, the Hebrew word for *honest* is *tzedek*. In another context, *tzedek* is the word for "justice." Justice itself depends on the use of honest measures. *Tzedek* is also the root word of *tzedakah,* usually—and mistakenly—translated as "charity." The underlying notion of helping others is the call for justice in the world—to right the scales, to bring up those brought low, to be compassionate toward others.

Counting

The root word of *accountability* is *count*.

I write this in the midst of being glued to the television set watching the Summer Olympics in Beijing, China. The athletes of the world have gathered in a spectacular celebration of summer sports that happens once every four years. Their success, their achievements, are judged; they are measured—their steps, laps, and leaps are counted.

Life, like sports, is about counting. In the business world, it is not uncommon to hear about "counting" gains or losses, wins and defeats.

We count the days of our lives, we count our birthdays, we count how many people we can invite to a wedding.

Like the Olympics, some of the most thrilling moments in life are not the individual achievements, but rather the team events. Swimmer

> Do you count on others? Do they count on you?

Michael Phelps, the most decorated Olympian in history, would not have won eight gold medals in the 2008 Olympic Games without the support of his teammates in two relay races. For Phelps, the relays were not simply a matter of counting hundredths of a second; the important question was this: Could he count on others to bring their best to the pool?

Do you count on others? Do they count on you?

Interestingly, there is a book of the Bible called Numbers. It begins with the census of the able-bodied males in the tribes who could be counted on to fight any enemies the Israelites might encounter during the Exodus. When Moses has completed the accounting, they total 603,550 (Numbers 1:46).

There is a wonderful commentary that points out that when you count the individual letters of each word in the Hebrew Bible, there are exactly 603,550! The scroll of the Five Books of Moses that is read in the synagogue is handwritten by specially trained scribes who take up to a full year to complete a single copy. According to Jewish law, if one letter of the 603,550 letters is missing, the entire Torah scroll is considered *pasul*— unfit for use.

Who is counting on you?

Every one of us counts.

And when we count, and when we can be counted on …

Then we become a blessing.

As Good as Gold

Accountability, honesty, and trust are not always about numbers.

Words count.

Warren Buffett, the world's greatest investor, reads balance sheets the way you and I read the morning paper. It is said that he has an encyclopedic memory, capable of recalling figures from complicated accounting. And yet, when it comes to making a deal, Buffett relies on something much more valuable than numbers.

In 1983, Buffett wanted to buy the most successful furniture store in America—the Nebraska Furniture Mart. The Mart was founded by the legendary Rose Blumkin, whose no-nonsense straight talk came with a thick Russian accent. Known by one and all in Omaha as "Mrs. B," she was a short fireplug of a woman, standing no taller than four-feet-eight, with a tight bun of jet-black hair. Mrs. B built the largest volume furniture retail outlet in the United States by offering her customers enormous selection, immediate delivery, and, most important, her mantra: "Sell Cheap and Tell the Truth."

Buffett had tried to buy the Mart once before, but he was turned down by Mrs. B, who deemed the offer "too cheap." On the day he succeeded, the deal went down like something out of a novel. Mrs. B was too short to walk comfortably around the store, which had grown to 200,000 square feet of retail space; instead, she puttered around in an electric golf cart. After tracking her down in the carpeting department, Mrs. B's favorite domain, Buffett began his pitch:

"Mrs. B, I want to buy the store."

"How much you gonna pay?" Mrs. B replied.

"Sixty million dollars," Buffett said.

Mrs. B stuck out her stubby little hand.

"Okay, Mr. Buffett, vee gotta deal."

No accountants. No lawyers. Just a simple handshake.

When your word is as good as gold, you conduct your business faithfully.

To Tell the Truth

You shall not give false testimony against your neighbor.

Exodus 20:16

One of my favorite television shows as a kid was *To Tell the Truth*. The moderator, Bud Collyer, would introduce three people who claimed to practice some interesting profession or to have achieved something extraordinary. Two of the people were imposters; one was sworn "to tell the truth." A panel of celebrities asked questions of the three contestants. The better the two imposters lied, the better the chances of fooling the judges. After a series of questions and answers, Collyer would ask the person telling the truth to stand up. After some feinting, the truth-teller would rise, often much to the surprise of the panelists and the audience.

It is so easy to present yourself as someone you are not. Stories of enhanced resumes, doctored diplomas, and assumed identities are common. Profiles on dating services are notorious for their inaccuracies. Photos of celebrities are airbrushed to perfection, not to mention the widespread popularity of all sorts of plastic surgery.

Distrust is rampant in the land. A recent Gallup poll of Americans indicated that 32 percent did not trust the government always (or even "most of the time") to do the right thing.

Truthiness

Fast forward to 2005 and the debut episode of a popular satirical television program, *The Colbert Report*. Comedian Stephen Colbert, playing the part of a conservative pundit, introduced a segment called "The Word" in which a new word would be coined. The first word: *truthiness*. What is *truthiness*? Essentially, it describes a person who claims to know the truth intuitively without regard to the facts.

Colbert explained:

> I will speak to you in plain, simple English. And that brings us to tonight's word: truthiness. Now, I'm sure some of the "word police," the "wordinistas" over at Webster's, are gonna say, "Hey, that's not a word." Well, anyone who knows me knows I'm no fan of dictionaries or reference books.

> I don't trust books. They're all fact, no heart. And that's exactly what's pulling our country apart today. 'Cause face it, folks: We are a divided nation. Not between Democrats and Republicans, or conservatives and liberals, or tops and bottoms. No, we are divided between those who think with their head and those who know with their heart.

> Consider Harriet Miers. If you "think" about it, of course her nomination [as Supreme Court justice] is absurd. But the president [George W. Bush] didn't say he "thought" about his selection. He said this: "I know her heart." Notice how he said nothing about her brain? He didn't have to. He feels the truth about Harriet Miers.

> And what about Iraq? If you think about it, maybe there are a few missing pieces to the rationale for war. But doesn't taking Saddam out feel like the right thing?

Colbert had struck a chord. Within days, the word gained currency around water coolers and newsrooms. Articles and television commentaries were written about the "truth of truthiness." Merriam-Webster announced that it was voted "Word of the Year" for 2006, outscoring *google* 5–1.

The original script for that broadcast on October 17, 2005, called for the word *truth,* but Colbert decided that it wasn't ridiculous enough. He told a reporter from *Newsweek* magazine: "We're not talking about truth, we're talking about something that seems like truth—the truth we want to exist."

No wonder so many of us question whether governments, the news media, and politicians are telling the truth.

Doubt

In his Pulitzer Prize–winning play *Doubt,* John Patrick Shanley explores the perils of "truth" based on feelings. Armed with flimsy circumstantial evidence, Sister Aloysius Beauvier suspects her supervisor, Father Brendan Flynn, of serious wrongdoing. It is unclear whether or not the priest has committed the crime. Father Flynn confronts her: "You haven't the slightest proof of anything!" She responds: "But I have my certainty!"

Ninety-nine Percent

John Edwards, a former senator from North Carolina and a candidate for president of the United States in 2008, confessed to cheating on his widely admired wife, Elizabeth, who suffers from terminal cancer. Explaining why he lied to his family, his staff, and mainstream reporters who took him at his word when he denied the allegation uncovered by a tabloid newspaper reporter, Edwards said: "I started to believe that I was special and became increasingly egocentric and narcissistic." And then he addressed the issue of honesty:

> I recognized my mistake and I told my wife that I had a liaison
> with another woman, and I asked for her forgiveness. Although I
> was honest in every painful detail with my family, I did not tell
> the public. When a supermarket tabloid told a version of the

story, I used the fact that the story contained many falsities to deny it. But, being 99 percent honest is no longer enough.

John Edwards, August 8, 2008

Being 99 percent honest is no longer enough.

This incredulous statement from a successful attorney, a senator, a potential president of the United States.

The Price of Dishonesty

Our great biblical figures were not immune to the seductiveness of power that can lead to dishonesty. And yet the genius of the Bible is to demonstrate how there is always a price to pay for lying.

Consider the story of Jacob. He is the second of twin boys born to Isaac and Rebekah, emerging from the womb "holding on to the heel of Esau," his older brother. His Hebrew name—*Ya'akov*—is a play on the word *heel*. Clearly, the Bible is signaling that Jacob wanted desperately to be first from the very moment of birth.

> There is always a
> price to be paid
> for lying.

In the Near East, the firstborn inherited the leadership of the family. Although Isaac favors Esau, Jacob makes two attempts to wrest away the birthright from his brother. In the first instance, Jacob tricks Esau into selling his birthright for a bowl of stew when he returns famished from a hunt. Even so, Isaac is determined to give his blessing to Esau, telling him to prepare a meal. Enter Rebekah, who acts to ensure that her favorite son, Jacob, will become the heir. She instructs Jacob to pretend to be Esau by donning hairy skins and presenting his father with a meal she prepares. Isaac is "old with eyes too dim to see" when the drama unfolds as Jacob delivers the meal to his father:

> He [Jacob] went to his father and said, "Father." And he [Isaac] said, "Yes, which of my sons are you?" Jacob said to his father, "I am Esau, your firstborn; I have done as you told me. Pray sit up and eat of my game, that you may give me your innermost blessing." Isaac said to his son, "How did you succeed so quickly, my

son?" And he [Jacob] said, "Because the Lord your God granted me good fortune." Isaac said to Jacob, "Come closer that I may feel you, my son—whether you are really my son Esau or not." So Jacob drew close to his father Isaac, who felt him and wondered, "The voice is the voice of Jacob, yet the hands are the hands of Esau." He did not recognize him, because his hands were hairy like those of his brother Esau; and so he blessed him. He asked, "Are you really my son Esau?" And when he said, "I am," he said, "Serve me and let me eat of my son's game that I may give you my innermost blessing."

Genesis 27:18–25

Jacob is lying. He is lying about who he is. He is lying about how he "succeeded" so quickly in the hunt. In fact, he compounds the lie by crediting "your God" with his good fortune. Does Isaac suspect that he is being had? Perhaps. He recognizes Jacob's voice, yet the disguise apparently works. Even so, Isaac asks a second time: "Are you really my son Esau?" And Jacob lies again.

There is another way to translate Isaac's first question of Jacob. The literal translation is not "Which of my sons are you?"; it is, "Who *are* you, my son?"

Who are you ... when you lie to another? Who are you ... when you are reduced to falsehoods to get what you want? Who are you ... when you are not honest ... with others ... or with *yourself*?

Jacob spends the rest of his life considering this question. Later in his life, he prepares to meet Esau, nervous that his brother will exact a terrible revenge. Jacob wrestles with an "angel of God" on that fateful night, surviving the fight, but emerging with a profound limp. His name is changed from *Ya'akov* to *Yisra-El*, "the one who wrestles with God." He is lied to by his sons, who, having sold the favored brother Joseph into slavery, tell him that a wild beast killed him, breaking Jacob's heart. Jacob/Israel pays a price for his lies.

There is always a price to be paid for lying.

Business Is War

My late uncle, Morton Friedlander, was the sweetest man in the world—at home. He was soft-spoken, loved to laugh, and adored his kids and wife. But when he went to work, he turned into a completely different person, a ferocious, hard-driving boss. Uncle Mort would head to the family-run grocery store, Louis Market, driving north on 52nd Street, whistling all the while … until he turned west on Military Avenue. He would spot the huge marquee, his face would turn flush, nostrils flaring. It was almost a Jekyll-and-Hyde kind of transformation.

Uncle Mort used to drive his employees crazy. He was forever tinkering with the displays. "Build it here," he would yell at Mancuso, one of the stock boys. And Mancuso and his crew would build an enormous display of toilet paper. This could take a couple of hours. Meanwhile, Uncle Mort would move to the front of the store, hustling the sackers from checkout counter to checkout counter. When Mancuso would come to tell him that the display was built, Uncle Mort would take one look at it and yell, "I don't like it. Move it!!!," pointing at another spot nearby, and Mancuso and crew would begin all over again.

Well before the days of computerized cash registers, the checkout clerks needed to memorize the prices on produce that could not be stamped. Uncle Morton loved to check whether a clerk knew the price of an item by heart. The clerks, all women, were terrified of him. One would be ringing up sales and, like a cat, he would quietly sneak up behind her and then yell into her ear at the top of his lungs, "Green beans!?!" This would scare her half to death! But when he came home, he turned from a tiger into a pussycat.

I once asked him about this change in him and he said, "Ronnie, it's a war out there. Business is war."

This reminds me of a story my rabbi, Ed Feinstein, tells about one of his professors at the rabbinical seminary. One day, the professor asked his students, "What is the most important section of the Torah?" The students engaged in a spirited debate: Was it the Ten Commandments, the stories of Genesis, the Exodus from Egypt? "No," the professor said. "The most important section is the first chapter of the portion *Ki Teitzei*, which begins, "When you go to war …"

When you go to war against your enemies, and the Lord your
God delivers them into your power and you take some of them
captive, and among the captives is a beautiful woman and you
desire her and would take her as your wife, you shall bring her
into your house, and she shall trim her hair, pare her nails, and
discard her captive's garb. She shall spend a month's time in your
house lamenting her father and mother; after that, you may come
to her and possess her, and she shall be your wife. Then, should
you no longer want her, you must release her outright. You must
not sell her for money; since you had your will of her, you must
not enslave her.

Deuteronomy 21:10–14

Why, the students wondered, is this the most important lesson in the
Bible?

The professor taught his lesson: "It is easy to be moral, honest, and caring in the comfort of your home, at the desk in your study, in your private
thoughts. Everyone thinks of herself or himself
as a good person. But when you are in the midst
of battle, when human beings often do awful
things, the real question of character is answered.
The Torah wants you to respect the woman's dig-
nity, to allow her to mourn the loss of her parents whom she will surely
not see again, to not be enslaved. This reflects the core value of the Israelite
religion—every human being is made in the image of God."

> **Was I honest?**
> _____
> BERNICE WOLFSON

"Business is war." The first question you're asked in heaven asks you to
think about your morality in the real world, in the marketplace, in the
tough competitive environment of business with all its conflicts, passions,
and crises.

The medieval commentator Rashi notes that the Hebrew word for *enemies*—*oyvecha*—is in the plural. Why wouldn't the text read "when you
go to meet your *enemy*?" There is the flesh-and-blood enemy standing
opposite you on the battlefield. But, there is another enemy—the heart-
and-soul enemy deep inside you, the impulse to abandon the rules of
decency and give in to lust, greed, and hate. The Bible is teaching the soul
of ethical behavior, even in the most chaotic environment imaginable.

Rabbi Feinstein makes the point: You know what business does to us. How many souls wither in certain businesses? How many of us are literally dying while making a living?

The Torah is teaching that by preserving the dignity of the other, you are preserving your own. What is at stake is not just the humanity of the other, but your own. Are you honest in the competitive world of business? Are you honest with your customers, fair with your clients, and gracious to your competitors? But, more important, are you honest with yourself, faithful to your own principles? Are you loyal to the best that you can be?

Was I Honest?

I grew up in a family business. My grandfather, Louis Paperny, and his four sons-in-law built one of the first modern supermarkets in Omaha, Nebraska. Louie—everyone called him "Louie"—began selling fruits and vegetables from a roadside stand. Louie had four daughters; the baby is my mother, Bernice. She was supposed to be a boy—and Zadie Louie treated her like one. At a young age, he would take her with him to the produce market very early in the morning. She learned many lessons from her father, who was known throughout the town as a man of integrity, a man whose word was his bond.

Mom has the business gene. She loves the thrill of retail—the give-and-take, the urge to serve, the interaction with customers. And, of course, the drive to make money. I am fond of saying, "If Mom hasn't counted a cash register, it hasn't been a good day." In the early 1960s, she applied for a Mr. Donut franchise—and was turned down because she was a woman. So she created her own doughnut shop—Dippy Donuts—which was an instant hit. Eventually, she had twelve locations in and around Omaha. After she sold the doughnut shops, she opened a deli, a bar, and a ladies' consignment clothing store.

When I asked Mom what questions she would be asked in heaven, she hesitated at first and then said: "Was I a good parent? A good wife? A good sister? A good daughter?"

"That's good," I replied. "What else?"

She thought a minute and said, "Was I honest?"

The First Question

Honesty, truth, faithfulness—these are the bedrock values of a life well lived.

Honesty, truth, faithfulness—these are the bedrock characteristics of relationships.

Be honest with others.

Be truthful with yourself.

Be faithful with your God.

On the next page, I invite you to reflect on your answers to the First Question you're asked in heaven.

Have you been honest with others, truthful with yourself, and faithful with your God?

2

The Immortality of Influence

Have you heard the term *footprint*? In the conversation about climate change, you often hear discussion about our *carbon footprint* or the *footprint* of a particular building. The term refers to the impact the activity or structure has on the environment—what is left as a result of the project.

What is your footprint on earth? What impact has your presence made in the world? What will you leave behind?

In other words, what is your *legacy*?

This is the meaning of the Second Question you're asked in heaven. In Rava's imagination, you are asked:

> *Asakta b'friyah u'riviyah?*
> Did you busy yourself with procreation?
>
> Shabbat 31a

Rava is thinking about the very first words God says to human beings:

> And God created human beings in the image of God;
> male and female God created them.
> God blessed them and God said to them:
> Be fruitful and multiply, fill the earth ...
>
> Genesis 1:27–28

Notice that the words are expressed as a blessing. Having children is a blessing. No one understands this better than those who are unable to conceive.

In America, approximately 10 percent of couples who try to get pregnant cannot. In all likelihood, this number will grow as the median age of marriage continues to rise and the peak years of fertility are bypassed. The challenge to get pregnant is so daunting that an entire industry has developed to help couples who have tried for one year unsuccessfully—the clinical definition of *infertility*. Tens of millions of dollars annually are spent on in vitro fertilization (current cost for one attempt: $10,000) and other techniques to help couples conceive and realize their dream of having a baby.

> Children are our lasting legacy. If we have done our job well as parents, they embody our values, our beliefs. They are our "footprint" in the world.

Psychologically, the inability to get pregnant is devastating. As my colleague Rabbi Elliot Dorff observes, every month is a final exam. Hopes are raised … and dashed. Self-esteem suffers, pressure in a marriage increases, everything revolves around precise timing, even the romance of trying disappears. There is a feeling of *letdown*—letting down yourself, letting down your partner, letting down parents who hope to be grandparents, letting down your faith community. Listen to Lisa:

> I couldn't stand to be in the presence of other young mothers with their babies. I would walk through the mall and avoid the maternity store. If a television commercial for diapers or baby food came on, I'd turn it off.

Elliot makes the point that a mitzvah (commandment) is only a mitzvah if a person can perform it. If a Jewish couple cannot conceive, it is not considered an "obligation." He advises infertile couples to find other ways to bring children into their lives.

For some who have tried everything, adoption is an option. But this can be a difficult process, drawn out and expensive. Some employ a surrogate, but this, too, can be fraught with complications and challenges. Others find ways to be foster parents or Big Brothers and Big Sisters.

And yet, the desire to have children is so strong, so compelling …

Why?

The answer gets to the heart of why Rava's question is so ... well ... pregnant.

In addition to the joys ... and, yes, the *oys* ... of raising kids, children are our lasting legacy. They represent continuity—continuity of family and community. They are the next chapter in our story. If we have done our job well as parents, they embody our values, our beliefs. They are our "footprint" in the world.

Maybe that's why the hospital takes a footprint on the birth certificate!

All My Children

On Sukkot last year, I visited a homeless shelter with a group of families from the Orange County Federation in Southern California. The Isaiah House is sponsored by Catholic Worker, an organization whose mission is to serve poor people with dignity. Located in Santa Ana's eastside barrio on Cypress Street, this beautifully restored Victorian home is open to those who are forgotten and lonely. Hospitality and respectful personal attention are at the heart of this remarkable service.

Isaiah House serves 3,500 hot meals every week, offers shelter for homeless families and women, and provides bags of food and clothing, showers, emergency assistance, a relaxing backyard, and always a friendly ear and kind words of support.

The house is led by Leia and Dwight Smith, a couple who left success-ful corporate careers to live in the home, a couple who decided long ago not to have their own children. Instead, they devote their lives to the hun-dreds of people who come through Isaiah House each week. As Leia explains:

We decided to commit our lives to serving the poor. In a way, the 120 women and children we invite into our home each night are our children; they are our family.

I believe people are created good, by nature are good, and seek to do good. What's lacking is not a desire or impulse, but an opportunity to do good.

I also think people respond to people, and not necessarily to programs. It's about human lives.... We have ideas about "the homeless." Responding to another human being is our truly human response ... going person to person is what creates meaning in the world. Things provide some pleasure perhaps, but they don't provide happiness, they don't provide what lasts. As it is said, "Nobody on their deathbed ever asks to be able to work longer." People ask if they could have more time with their family. That's what we all really want.

The Best Boy in the United States of America

I am Louie Paperny's legacy.

My grandfather was a larger-than-life figure, although he only stood, maybe, five feet tall. Stocky of build, with an expressive face featuring sparkling blue bug-eyes and an always-ruddy complexion, Louie was stronger than an ox. His early years as a fruit and vegetable peddler lugging heavy sacks of potatoes in his adopted hometown of Omaha, Nebraska, endowed him with huge arms and legs. And yet, he was one of the most gentle human beings, a man who wore his emotions on his sleeve—a man who cried at the drop of a hat and, certainly, at the sight of a grandchild.

I called him "Zadie," a Yiddish term of endearment.

Zadie loved three things: his family, his business, and his adopted country, the United States of America. I never, ever heard Zadie say in his thick Russian accent "the United States." It was always "the United States of America." He never spoke of his life in Russia—it was always a deep, dark secret, a mystery. To this day, my mother barely knows anything about his family or his life in Minsk. It was as if the minute he arrived in America, he wanted to forget where he had come from. He embraced the freedom, the opportunity that America afforded him. The fact that he was able to raise a family and build a successful business and enjoy a level of affluence he never believed possible—all this he credited to the United States of America, "the greatest country in the world."

Zadie had a big, overstuffed chair in his living room, where he sat like a king. As a young boy visiting Zadie, the instant I rounded the corner into the living room, I made a beeline for him, sitting on his throne. As I rushed into his arms, he would cross his powerful legs behind me, locking me in a tight embrace from which there was absolutely no escape. I would wriggle to try to get out of his grasp, but it was no use. When I settled down into his loving hug, he would give me a big, sloppy kiss, look me in the eye, and say, "Ronnie, you're the best boy in the United States of America!" Everyone knew that Louie Paperny's word was true and as good as gold. So there was no question, no doubt in my mind, that I, in fact, *was* the best boy in the United States of America.

> Parenting is a career, just as much as lawyering or doctoring or engineering or anything else. And it gives as much meaning to life as anything else we can possibly do on this earth.

Can you imagine hearing that you are the best boy in the United States of America? Can you imagine what this did for my developing self-esteem?

But when my brother Bobby ran into Zadie's arms, and he was ensnared in Zadie's dreaded/beloved leglock, and when Zadie gave him a big, sloppy kiss, and when Zadie looked him in the eye and said, "Bobby, you're the best boy in the United States of America!"— it mattered not. When brother Dougie ran into Zadie's arms, and was ensnared in Zadie's dreaded/beloved leglock, and when Zadie gave him a big, sloppy kiss, and when Zadie looked him in the eye and said: "Dougie, you're the best boy in the United States of America!"—it mattered not. Somehow, all nine of us grandchildren believed Zadie when he anointed each one of us the "best boy" or "best girl" in the United States of America.

Life after Death

Although there is a notion of a physical life after death in Judaism, the Rabbis of the Talmud struggled with an idea that was impossible to prove. They certainly did not expect or prepare for an immediate physical reincarnation. No elaborate tombs laden with objects the dead might need in the afterlife. The Jewish burial calls for a simple wooden coffin, the body wrapped in a plain white linen shroud, a shroud with no pockets. Whatever you accumulated in your life on earth was left behind. You literally can't take it with you.

What do you leave behind? Money, possessions, artifacts? Perhaps. But, the Rabbis knew there was something far more valuable, far more important remaining on earth.

Your children. Your grandchildren.

They are your legacy.

Zadie died in 1974, thirty-five years ago … and yet, hardly a day goes by that I don't think of him. I even look a little like him. I have the same ruddy complexion that makes it appear as if I were blushing all the time. I have his sparkling blue eyes. Some say I have his entrepreneurial spirit, his love of family, and his deep respect for the United States of America.

In the summer of 2008, I visited his grave in Omaha. I don't know what you do when you visit a gravesite, but I talk to the deceased. Not out loud … and no, I don't expect a response. I'm unsure if Zadie's soul "hears" me, and, in a way, it doesn't matter. It comforts me to remember him by sharing my life's story, as I place a stone on his marker, a reminder that I was there.

On this latest visit, I told Zadie about our daughter Havi's wedding to Dave, and Michael's success in Internet advertising, and our recent trip abroad. I gave him a health update on Mom and Dad. I thought he'd be tickled that I teach about his practice of welcoming his customers at the grocery store as a model for congregational leaders. And I shared with him how thrilled I was to give the High Holiday sermon at Temple Israel in Omaha, Nebraska, as the entire congregation read my book, *God's To-Do List*. I even told him that an African-American man had a very good chance of becoming the president of the United States of America.

And then I stood there, picturing him in my thoughts, remembering him in my heart. Finally, I said a little prayer: "I hope someday soon, I'll get to lock a grandchild between my legs, and I'll get to give her or him a big, sloppy kiss, and I'll get to say: 'You're the best boy … or … you're the best girl in the United States of America.'"

Who's at the Airport?

My friend Rabbi Jack Riemer tells the story of meeting a young female attorney on a flight to attend a family event in Berkeley, California. Somehow, the conversation came around to children.

"I don't want any," she said, "and I don't intend to have any. My husband agrees with me, but we are constantly getting pressure from our parents and from other people. And we don't like it. What arguments are there—what valid arguments—not just social pressures, for having children?"

We summed up the reasons for not having them. That was easy: the loss of freedom, the expense, the worry, the inevitability of disappointed expectations, and above all—the need to put yourself second at least for some years.

"But look at the advantages you could give your children," I said timidly.

"That's only a reason for someone who is already convinced. What's that to me?" was her answer.

"You know how lonely the childless become as they age. Children keep you young," I said.

"Oh, sure," she said. "The next thing you'll tell me is that suffering is good for the soul."

We stopped the abstract talk. The only logical arguments for having children are social, and we had agreed to rule social arguments out of the discussion. So we hung up there in the air, seeking some convincing logic, not sure where it was. Her tone softened.

"Why did you have children?" she asked.

Love had something to do with it, I knew, but I couldn't say how. I like kids in general, and mine in particular, but there is something selfish in my love for my children. They somehow help fit me into time. Perhaps that was it, finally: Without children, we are flashes in the pan, here today and gone tomorrow. With children, we belong on earth and we have a future and a past. Our children put us into the continuum of life.

We talked of parents, then: mine close; hers not.

"You must feel very much alone," I said.

"We are all alone," she answered.

The flight was over. We both smiled, and shrugged as we unbuckled our seat belts and reached up for our luggage, knowing that reasons are ultimately rationalizations. We knew we would never see each other again, we smiled, shouldered our suitcases, and walked off the plane.

She headed purposefully toward the rental cars ... by herself.

I walked up the ramp toward my daughter, who was waiting ... for me.

That scene—of one person heading toward a rental car and the other toward a daughter who was smiling—says it all. Reasons can be reasoned with, but this experience cannot be traded for anything. Parenting is a career, just as much as lawyering or doctoring or engineering or anything else. And it gives as much meaning to life as anything else we can possibly do on this earth.

Investing in Your Family

Let's look more carefully at Rava's question.

It is not: "Did you *love* your family?"

It is not: "Did you *give* your children everything?"

It is not: "Did you *leave* a lot of money in your will?"

It is: "Did you *invest* yourself in your family?"

The Aramaic word is *asakta*—literally, did you *busy* yourself with your family? Did you spend time with your family?

Rabbi Harold Kushner once said that, on a deathbed, no one ever wishes she had spent more time on her business.

This question asks:

Did you spend enough time with your family?

Investing in Memories

I read once about a man named Ron Stefanski of Ann Arbor, Michigan, who, despite a severe economic downturn rattling the country, bought his family a thirty-eight-foot sailboat. Was this the right thing to do? Wouldn't the $55,000 spent on the boat purchase be better used in a college fund for his two teenage boys?

Listen to Ron's reasoning, as reported by Ron Lieber in the *New York Times:*

> When you look at life ... it's about creating memories. [My wife Kay and I] are getting ready to be empty-nesters, learning how to navigate the space of being alone together ... having the boat is an opportunity to connect, to spend time together. The fact that we have to put the effort into driving up to the lake, it marks the time as untouchable.

How do you invest in your family?

Bruce and Pam Friedlander invest in a weekly Friday night dinner with their family. Complete with favorite foods and the traditional Shabbat ritual around the table, their kids and grandkids look forward to this time together with "Pa" and "B." Candles are lit, grape juice is drunk, and homemade challah is eagerly chowed down. After dinner, Jack and Joe lead the singing of songs learned at their preschool. They have turned Friday night into family night.

Judy and Louis Miller invest by hosting their entire immediate family for an annual vacation during the winter holidays. For twelve consecutive years, the Millers, their adult children, and their grandchildren have enjoyed two weeks together eating, swimming, and visiting with each other. The first family trip was to Israel; Hawaii is also a favorite destination. When asked why they do it, Judy says, "Bonding. Our kids and grandkids have such a wonderful time together. Our hope is they'll be close. All we're doing is making memories that will last a lifetime."

No More Questions, Your Honor

The idea of a Heavenly Court is found in the pages of the Zohar, the classic text of Kabbalah, the Jewish mystical tradition. Every person stands before the bench to answer questions about his life on earth. Like other courts, this one features a "prosecuting attorney" who brings evidence against him and a "defense attorney" who argues for his admission to heaven. After listening to the questioning, God the Judge intervenes and asks, "Did you raise your children properly?"

If the answer is "yes," God refuses to hear any more testimony against the person and immediately welcomes him in.

Just before we walked our daughter Havi down the aisle at her wedding to Dave, our immediate family members gathered in a room at the Desert Springs Resort to participate in the ancient Jewish tradition called *bedeken.* The word literally means "veiling," recalling the biblical incident when Jacob thinks he's marrying his beloved Rachel, daughter of Laban, but instead is married to Rachel's older sister, Leah. How did that little mistake happen? Laban wanted to ensure that his elder daughter, Leah, was married first. So he disguised her identity with a veil and Jacob was tricked. The *bedeken* ceremony is an opportunity for the groom to "veil" his bride, to make sure he is getting the right girl.

> **What was your legacy?**
> ──────────────
> BEV WEISE

At Dave and Havi's *bedeken,* Rabbi Ed Feinstein explained the significance of the ritual and then turned to the young couple. He asked both of them if they were prepared to enter the sacred covenant of marriage. He had each of them sign the marriage document, the *ketubah.* And then, Rabbi Feinstein said something so remarkable, something so real and so true that it gave me goose bumps:

> You are surrounded by your family and friends who love you, who raised you, and have brought you to this moment. But, from now on, you are no longer only a descendant. From now on, you have the potential to be an ancestor.

How to Be an Ancestor

And what is the life task of an ancestor?

It is to transmit your values, beliefs, and culture from your generation to the next.

You become a teacher.

How?

The answer is found in the *Ve'ahavta* prayer:

> Love the Lord Your God with all your heart, with all your soul, and with all your might. And these words which I command you

this day, you shall take to heart. You shall diligently teach them to your children. You shall recite them at home and away, morning and night. You shall bind them as a sign upon your hand; they shall be a reminder above your eyes, and you shall inscribe them on the doorposts of your homes and upon your gates.

Notice that there are three steps:

1. *You love God completely.* With all your heart. With all your soul. With all your might.

   You cannot teach what you do not know. You cannot share your beliefs if you don't know what you believe. You cannot talk the talk unless you walk the walk.

   Kids see right through adults. They know when you're faking it. They know whether you feel strongly about something or not. Kids don't just listen to what you *say*; they watch what you *do*. "Action speaks louder than words." A cliché, perhaps, but undeniably true.

   So get your act together. Figure out your theology. Pay attention to the Third Question (we'll get there in a moment). Equip yourself to be the best ancestor-teacher you can be.

2. *Create a teaching environment.* Have you ever been in a dynamic, exciting, stimulating classroom? The space is filled with learning. Lessons spill out from bulletin boards, blackboards, computer screens, library shelves, and projects. Everywhere you turn, there are things to learn. Ancestor-teachers know how to create homes where the values to be taught are literally on the doorposts of the house, a house set within the gates of a community. Ancestor-teachers share their lessons 24/7—at bedtime, mealtime, at work and at play, at home and away. Ancestor-teachers employ all sorts of learning strategies—reading, writing, cooking, surfing, building, singing, and more. Ancestor-teachers fill the home with joyous ritual, meaningful prayer, and purposeful projects to repair the world.

3. *Teach diligently.* What does it mean to teach "diligently"? It means to teach with intentionality. It means to teach with consistency. It means to teach with intensity.

Ultimately, to be an ancestor-teacher is to be a role model.

I am reminded of this every time I get on an airplane. Before takeoff, the flight attendants present a safety demonstration. They show you how to buckle your seat belt. They point out the emergency exits. They put on a life vest. They warn that you cannot smoke or use your cell phone. They ask you to be careful opening overhead bins because things may have shifted in flight.

And then they tell you what to do, God forbid, if the plane loses air pressure. Orange oxygen masks will fall from the ceiling and they demonstrate how to put one on. But they say something quite strange, unexpected.

If you are traveling with a child, who gets the mask first?

You do. You are told—rather forcefully—that if you are an adult sitting next to a child, you are to put your mask on first.

I don't buy it. No way. If I am on a plane with my child or grandchild … and there is a crisis … and those orange masks come falling down—every bone in my body, every instinct I have, is to put that mask on the child first. Agreed?

> Ancestors have, as my teacher Rabbi Harold Schulweis puts it so eloquently, the immortality of influence.

But, no. You are told to put your mask on first. You know why?

If the oxygen is not flowing to you, you cannot help the child. In fact, you could easily black out.

And, in a crisis, the child needs the model of the adult, to be reassured that putting on the mask is the right thing to do.

This is why I always encourage parents and grandparents to continue practicing home rituals, to continue going to worship services, even after the kids leave the house. Then, the message is this: "I did this for me. These are *my* candles. This is *my* prayer."

Ancestors have the oxygen flowing to them—*first.*

Ancestors love God—*first.*

Ancestors create value-able homes—*first.*

Ancestors engage in spiritual practices, for themselves—*first.*

Ancestors live the talk.

Ancestors invest in their families.

Ancestors have, as my teacher Rabbi Harold Schulweis puts it so eloquently, *the immortality of influence.*

Have children.

Adopt children.

Mentor children.

Teach children.

Leave a legacy.

You'll be asked about it in heaven.

On the next page, I invite you to reflect on your answers to the Second Question you're asked in heaven.

How are you creating your legacy?

3

Turn It ... and Turn It

Learn.

As someone who has spent his whole career as a teacher, I am thrilled with the Third Question.

> *Kava'ata itim la-Torah?*
> Did you set times for Torah?
> Shabbat 31a

From the moment of birth, we begin to learn. We take in the world around us and we learn. Our brain grows at a phenomenal pace and we begin to fill it with information, we learn skills, and we experience emotional highs and lows. Before our fifth birthdays, most of us begin formal study in school and, for at least the next twelve years, most of our waking hours are spent in one activity: learning.

So far, so good.

But then we graduate—high school, college, graduate school.

And we stop studying.

We leave the world of textbooks, lectures, labs, and exams, and we enter our professional lives—our very, very busy professional lives.

I once asked a friend whether he makes time for study.

"Study? Who has time to study? I barely have time to breathe between commuting to my job, working, coming home, grabbing some dinner, and then plopping in front of a TV or a computer before flopping into bed. And the next morning I get up and do it all over again."

Sound familiar?

On the Same Page

Let's look at the Third Question more carefully.

The two key phrases are *kava'ata itim* and *la-Torah*.

Kava'ata itim means "to set times." To schedule. To make a date. To establish a regular, appointed time.

We do this all the time. Our calendars are filled with appointments: business meetings, coffee with friends, social dates. We set times to do things almost every day.

Rava just wants you to have an appointment to learn.

La-Torah is literally translated as "for Torah." The meaning is "for the study of Torah."

The word *Torah* itself has multiple meanings. The root is *yud-raish-hei*, "to learn." It is the word for *Bible,* a term describing all of Jewish legal literature, and it can refer to the accumulated learning of a great scholar— for example, "I've been studying the Torah of Heschel." Rava, however, means Bible study.

I envy my Christian friends who set a time for daily Bible study. They don't go a day without cracking open their Bible and learning a verse or two. Some even engage in the spiritual practice of memorizing Bible verses.

The closest thing in the Jewish community is called *Daf Yomi*—literally, "the daily page." Thousands of Orthodox Jews study the same page of Talmud every day. You can see them on trains coming into New York City, with their heads deep into a book, studying a page, looking into a computer screen, or even listening to a *ShasPod,* an iPod loaded with lectures on all 2,711 pages of the Babylonian Talmud. Beginning with the first page and studying each consecutive folio, one full cycle of studying the *shisha sidrei* (the six orders of the Talmud), or *shas,* takes about seven years, five months. On the last day of studying the final page, huge gatherings are held around the world for a group celebration called a *siyuum,* the "conclusion." The eleventh cycle was completed on March 1, 2005, with an estimated 120,000 people participating, including a sold-out Madison Square Garden and dozens of locations around the world. On the very next day, March 2, 2005, the twelfth cycle began again at the first page of the first book of the Talmud. The scheduled completion date is August 22, 2012.

The Unbroken Cycle

This notion of the unbroken cycle of study is apparent in the celebration of the Simchat Torah holiday. The last verses of the Torah are read aloud in the synagogue and—without a break—the scrolls are turned back to the beginning and the first verses are read. In every synagogue in the world, selections from the same weekly portion of the Torah are read to the community. It may be the longest continuous community read-aloud in history—a set time for study.

This same idea explains why every book of the Talmud begins on page 2, not on page 1.

The Voices in the Library

When my friend David Wolpe became a rabbi, he was offered the position as librarian at what was then the University of Judaism, now the American Jewish University, in Los Angeles. The university is blessed with the Jack M. Ostrow Library, the largest collection of Jewish books on the West Coast, and David, a brilliant author himself, wanted to immerse himself in the atmosphere of a library.

At a fund-raising function for the Ostrow Library, I once heard David describe what he loved about his job. "I walk through the stacks—aisle upon aisle of volume after volume—and I don't *see* them as books— paper, ink, bindings. I *hear* them—as voices of authors who hope I will pick up their teaching and learn from their unique perspective. Each book, each author, each teacher calls to me. Ancient voices. Modern voices. Pick me. Go and learn."

The Never-Ending Conversation

Jews are known as the "People of the Book," but a more accurate term would be the "People of the Never-Ending Conversation." Since the day after the giving of the Torah on Mount Sinai, the Jewish people has been reading and studying and commenting on the Bible in what is likely the longest-running conversation among one people. And, amazingly, this conversation has been remembered and recorded for more than two thousand years.

As each generation of Rabbis studied the Torah—the Five Books of Moses, the Prophets, and the Writings (collectively known as Tanakh, an acronym for *Torah, Nevi'im, Ketuvim*)—they debated the meaning of virtually every word and phrase. The most famous of these Rabbis offered a running commentary on major books of the Bible. So, for example, Rabbi Shlomo Yitzhaki, known as Rashi (1040–1105 CE), completed his classic commentary on the Five Books of Moses in eleventh-century France, while in twelfth-century Egypt, Rabbi Moses ben Maimon, called Maimonides (1135–1204 CE), wrote his Mishneh Torah.

To facilitate comparison of the major commentaries, an unknown brilliant editor decided to create an edition of the Bible that features a small section of the biblical text, surrounded by the commentaries of Rashi, Tosafot, and others. Studying the Bible from such a text is like sitting at a table with these luminaries, an open Torah in the center, and, as each word or phrase is uttered out loud, the disparate voices chime in with their interpretations.

Another outstanding example of this phenomenon is the Talmud, a collection of conversations between Rabbi-scholars who shaped Jewish law as they debated the meaning of the Mishnah, the codification of Jewish law redacted in 200 BCE. As soon as the Mishnah was collected, groups of Rabbis in Babylonia and Jerusalem argued the meaning of the laws, bringing biblical citations as proof texts, in the part of the Talmud called Gemorrah. In a remarkably inclusive gesture, all of the comments (nearly two hundred years worth) of this diverse group of Rabbis are included in the Talmud, regardless of whether the final decision of how the law would be implemented went according to one or the other. So, although in debates between Rabbi Hillel and Rabbi Shammai, the law almost always follows Rabbi Hillel, Rabbi Shammai's minority opinion is recorded and studied, right alongside that of his colleague.

> Since the day after the giving of the Torah on Mount Sinai, the Jewish people has been reading and studying and commenting on the Bible in what is likely the longest-running conversation among one people. And, amazingly, this conversation has been remembered and recorded for more than two thousand years.

On a single folio of Talmud, these discussions are center page, surrounded by the writings of several commentators who weigh in with their interpretations of the text. Each commentator's voice is there on the page, for all to *see* and *hear*. Moreover, the classic form of Jewish text study, *chevrutah* (from the word *chaver*—"friend"), is for *two* students to sit face-to-face, open Talmud in front of each, reading aloud the text, then deciphering the commentaries, and finally debating between themselves how each understands the debate—in effect, adding to a centuries-old, never-ending conversation.

> Did you learn all
> you could?
>
> ───────────
>
> TED PLAVIN

Rabbi David Hartman, one of the great rabbinic educators of our time, recalls that as a boy in a yeshiva, someone came to the study hall one day asking for donations to support the celebration of the 750th anniversary of the death of Maimonides—the Rambam. The young Hartman looked up from his text and exclaimed: "The Rambam is dead? How can he be dead? He and I were arguing with each other just this morning!"

Turn It

In most synagogues, the worship service is conducted not just by the rabbi and cantor. There are opportunities for laypeople to lead the prayers or to participate in the rituals embedded in the experience. These "honors" are bestowed on regular attendees, guests celebrating life-cycle events, mourners remembering their departed loved ones, visiting scholars, and others.

Some of these honors are more challenging than others. For instance, the honor of lifting the Torah scroll from the reading table, called *hagbah*, can be a difficult task. The scroll itself—the entire Five Books of Moses—is handwritten on parchment with a quill pen and then attached to two long dowels. Depending on the size of the parchment and the dowels, the Torah scroll can be fairly light in weight or quite heavy. Complicating matters is the issue of when in the Torah reading cycle you receive the honor. For example, to lift the Torah scroll when the early portions of Genesis are read means you'd better have a strong left arm; most of the parchments are rolled up on the left dowel (Hebrew is read from right to left).

Moreover, experienced Torah lifters have learned the proper technique for the task. To achieve some leverage, the lifter moves the scroll to the edge of the reading table, just about halfway down the parchment, and then pushes down with the lower handles on the dowels and lifts straight up in a kind of weight-lifting move. I call this "pumping Torah."

Complicating matters further, since the congregation sings the words "*v'zot ha-Torah asher sahm Moshe lifnei b'nai Yisrael*—This is the Torah that Moses set before the people Israel," it is considered preferable for the lifter to show the worshippers as many columns of the Torah script as possible. Depending on the weight of the scroll, the time of year, and the lifter's available muscle power, a good *hagbah* can show three, four, even five columns. Six columns? You'll get an admiring *yasher koach*—literally "May you be strengthened," or more colloquially, "Way to go!" After achieving the appropriate "lift," the *hagbah* sits down, holding the scrolls together while another honoree—the *gelilah*—dresses the Torah scroll with its binding, mantle, and silver adornments.

> Through the study of Torah, by applying its lessons to our lives, we learn to make a living and to make a life well lived.

There is even some danger involved in lifting a Torah scroll. It is the only object in Judaism considered sacred—it represents the revelation on Mount Sinai, a gift from God—and it is never allowed to touch the ground. Even when placed on a table, a cloth or *tallit* (prayer shawl) is used to protect the scroll. When the Torah scroll is worn out, it is never thrown away; it is buried with the same respect accorded a dead person. When the Torah is lifted and when the ark is open, the congregation rises.

The worst, worst, *worst* thing that can happen in a synagogue is if a *hagbah* drops the Torah scroll. Even a slight fumble will evoke gasps from the congregation. Think of it; if you drop a prayer book or a copy of the English translation of the Torah on the floor, you are supposed to kiss it as a sign of respect. Imagine what happens if you witness a Torah scroll dropped to the ground!

Here's what happens. Even though the *hagbah* did the dropping, the entire congregation is responsible for the act and must engage in *tikkun*—"repair." A *tikkun* often follows a rule of thumb known as *mida k'neged mida,* meaning the remedy should fit the transgression. Since it took forty days to receive the Torah on Mount Sinai, everyone who saw the Torah scroll drop is to fast for forty days. Now that's a lot of fasting. So the rabbinic authorities decided that the forty days did not have to be in a row and would only include the daylight hours. Today, some rabbis suggest that forty people fast one day each, or, instead of fasting, ask the witnesses to offer *tzedakah* (righteous giving).

As serious as this is, sometimes funny things happen to those honored with *hagbah*. I was once asked to be *hagbah* at Rabbi Joel and Fredi Rembaum's youngest son's *brit milah* (ritual circumcision). The ceremony was held in their home during a Monday morning prayer service and the Torah portion was read. The Torah scroll was placed on their dining room table. Due to the low clearance in the room, I had to do a deep knee bend in order to get the leverage I needed to lift the scroll, without hitting the ceiling. Holding the ends of the dowels in each hand, I pushed down hard ... only to hear a frightening sound: "Riiiiiiiip." My pants had torn to pieces, exposing my rear end! That was the end of my Torah pumping days.

There is great symbolism in the Torah scroll. Since there are no punctuation marks and no page numbers on the parchments, the scroll must be rolled to the proper section to find the appointed reading for the day.

This reminds me of the great insight of Ben Bag Bag (yes, that's his real name), a Rabbi, in Pirke Avot:

> Turn it and turn it ... because everything is in it.
>
> Pirke Avot 5:24

Turn it. And turn it. Read it and read it. Over and over again. Each time you do, you will learn something new.

Friday Morning with Rabbi Lieber

When I first came to the University of Judaism in Los Angeles in 1974 as a student, I met the then-president, Rabbi David Lieber. A man of slight build, yet strong and fit, Dr. Lieber was building a first-class educational institution of higher Jewish learning on the West Coast. To do so, he needed programs, faculty, a facility, and the support of laypeople who would donate significant funding. To achieve the last of these goals, the university sponsored breakfasts in local synagogues and an annual dinner honoring a communal leader, and board members engaged in one-on-one solicitations.

Yet I believe the single most important activity that helped Dr. Lieber build the institution—now called American Jewish University—was a weekly Bible class on Friday mornings. Dr. Lieber, may his memory be a blessing, loved the Bible. His PhD dissertation was on the Psalms, he taught courses to the college students, and, after his retirement as president, he was the senior editor for the brilliant Conservative movement edition of the Torah, *Etz Hayim*. But it was his Friday morning Bible class that I will best remember.

For exactly one hour every Friday morning, David Lieber taught the Bible to some thirty devoted adults. Most of the regulars never missed a class in all those years. It was how Dr. Lieber taught that was so amazing. He began with the first verse of Genesis, translated it, commented on it, and invited questions about it until everyone had "turned it and turned it" … and then the group moved on to the next verse. Verse by verse. Every week. Until they reached the end of the Torah … and then … they started all over again. Over the course of more than thirty years, Dr. Lieber's Friday morning Bible class "turned" the Torah at least three times.

> **Prayer is how we talk with God. Study is how we hear God's voice.**

The students were so devoted, so appreciative of the patient and insightful teaching of Dr. Lieber, that they rallied to his cause: the building of the university. The largest donors and the most consistent givers were students of Dr. Lieber. It mattered not that they were all busy professionals, investors, and businesspeople. They loved him for his scholarship, his erudition, and most of all, his kindness as a teacher.

Rabbi Elazar ben Azariah teaches:

> *Im ein kemach, ein Torah.*
> *Im ein Torah, ein kemach.*
> If there is no flour, there is no study of Torah.
> If there is no study of Torah, there will be no flour.
>
> Pirke Avot 3:21

In other words, educational enterprises—for the young and not-so-young—must be supported if the study of Torah is to continue. And through the study of Torah, by applying its lessons to our lives, we learn to make a living and to make a life well lived.

Listening to God

People often ask about the meaning of prayer and study, two of the central activities of most religions.

I have always liked the simple, yet profound answer offered by Rabbi Louis Finkelstein:

> Prayer is how we talk with God.
> Study is how we hear God's voice.

What I've Learned

For the past few years, my good friend Craig Taubman, a contemporary composer and performer of Jewish music, has published a small book of daily reflections for reading during the month of Elul, leading up to the Jewish New Year. One year, the theme of his "Jewels for Elul" was learning. He asked me to write a short piece about "what I've learned" and from whom. I decided to think about my family members and what I've learned from them over the years. Here is my list:

> Zadie Louie: Greet everyone.
>
> Bubie Ida: Bake mandel bread.
>
> Grandma Celia: Soap operas rock.
>
> Mom Bernice: Always think about others.
>
> Dad Alan: Be creative.
>
> Zadie K.: Keep moving.
>
> Bubie K.: Laugh out loud.
>
> Uncle George: Love is popular; life is expensive.
>
> Aunt Ruth: Love—a bushel and a peck.

Uncle Leonard: Dream big.

Aunt Rose: Life's a bowl of Jell-O.

Uncle Ben: Invest.

Aunt Sylvia: Diamonds are a girl's best friend.

Uncle Mort: Work hard.

Susie: Family first.

Havi: Courage.

Michael: Just do it.

Brother Bob: Bad guys are out there.

Sister-in-Law Sibby: We'll get Bin-Laden ... eventually.

Niece Rebecca: Use your voice.

Nephew Alex: Use your talent.

Brother Doug: Love your children.

Sister-in-Law Sara: Heal.

Nephew Avi: Hug everyone.

Niece Naomi: Seek silence.

Nephew Aaron: Know statistics.

COUSINS:

Bruce: Get up, turn on news. If there's no bird flu, go back to bed.

Pam: Chant Torah.

Laurie: Take the stairs.

Mark: Work out.

Steve: Read books, then pass them on.

Linda: Take pictures.

Joanie: There is always hope.

Paul: Enjoy fine wine.

Bill: Fight.

Margo: *Fait ses valises* ("pack the suitcases").

Nancy: Grandparenting is the reward for having children.

Don: Pick the best fruit.

Family is your greatest teacher.

Who Is Wise?

In Pirke Avot, the *Sayings of the Ancestors,* one of my all-time favorite questions is asked by Rabbi Ben Zoma: "Who is wise?"

The answer:

> One who learns from all persons. As it is written: "From all my teachers have I gained understanding" (Psalm 119:99).
>
> Pirke Avot 4:1

Roots and Branches

For centuries, the debate has raged: What is more important—doing good deeds or studying?

In Pirke Avot, Rabbi Elazar ben Azariah seems to argue for good deeds.

> When a person's wisdom exceeds a person's good deeds, to what may one be compared? To a tree with many branches, but few roots. A wind blows, uproots it, and topples it over, as it is written: "One shall be like a desert shrub that never thrives but dwells unwatered in the wilderness, in a salty, solitary land" (Jeremiah 17:6).
>
> However, when a person's good deeds exceed a person's wisdom, to what may one be compared? To a tree with few branches but with many roots. All the winds of the world may blow against it, yet they cannot move it from its place, as it is written: "One shall be like a tree planted by the waters that spreads its roots by the stream. Untouched

> Did you live a life that furthered the covenantal mission of *Klal Yisrael* [the people of Israel] to enrich the world through the spread of Torah values?
>
> RICHARD JOEL, PRESIDENT, YESHIVA UNIVERSITY

by the scorching heat, its foilage remains luxurious. It will have no concern in a year of drought and will not cease from bearing fruit" (Jeremiah 17:8).

Pirke Avot 3:22

In the Talmud, a different answer is given:

These are the deeds that yield immediate fruit ["spiritual reward"] and continue to yield fruit in the world to come:

Honoring parents
Deeds of loving-kindness
Setting a time for study—morning and evening
Providing hospitality
Visiting the sick
Helping the needy bride
Attending a funeral
Probing the meaning of prayer
Making peace between one person and another, and between husband and wife
And the study of Torah is the most important of them all.
Talmud torah k'neged kulam.

Shabbat 127a

Why is study of Torah the most important?
   It is only through study that we learn *how* to do the other good deeds.
   Nevertheless, the purpose of the study of Torah is to do good deeds.
   Study.
   Then, do.
   Set a time for study … and live a life well lived.

On the next page, I invite you to reflect on your answers to the Third Question you're asked in heaven.

How are you learning?

4

The Hope of God

The Fourth Question you're asked in heaven is not about your accomplishments, your values, or your legacy.
It is about your attitude.

> *Tzipita li'yeshuah?*
> Did you hope for deliverance?
>
> Shabbat 31a

Did you live with hope in your heart?

Examining the Heart

There is a thin line between hope and fear.

On a Monday morning, as Susie lay on a hospital gurney awaiting a procedure to determine whether she had heart trouble, my mind raced between the two emotions.

We had recently returned from a long journey overseas where I taught in Hong Kong, Australia, and New Zealand. Susie had done well on the flights, but she had been unable to walk through the airports without an acute shortness of breath. I knew this was a symptom of heart disease and I convinced her that she needed to address the problem as soon as we returned to Los Angeles. It was then that she confided in me how poorly she was feeling; yet she feared finding out the true cause.

A longtime type 2 diabetic, Susie began a series of tests ordered by her doctors. Any number of consequences of this silent disease could be contributing to her lethargy. In short order, she had an MRI of the brain, a CT scan of her gastrointestinal tract and lungs, and a series of blood tests. But after the cardiologist reviewed her electrocardiogram, the doctor forcefully recommended an immediate angiogram to investigate whether Susie had blockages in her heart arteries. And so she awaited the test that would examine the inside of her heart that Monday morning at Kaiser Permanente Sunset.

You don't know what to hope for. And you are darn sure afraid.

As I sat in the waiting room near the heart catheterization lab, my mind vacillated between the twin poles of hope and fear. I hoped they wouldn't find anything. But, then, what was causing her poor health? So I hoped they *would* find something. And if they did find a blockage, I hoped the doctors would be able to balloon the artery, pushing the plaque against the arterial walls and opening the flow of blood to the heart. But what if they couldn't? What if they found blockages like the ones discovered in my cousin Bruce's heart a year earlier, blockages that could not be fixed with a balloon, blockages that could only be bypassed, necessitating open-heart surgery? Open-heart surgery on a fifty-eight-year-old woman, my beloved wife of thirty-eight years?!? I knew the risks of open-heart surgery; my father and father-in-law have had multiple heart procedures. The image of Susie with a "zipper," a scar down the middle of her chest, enduring the ventilator tube in the throat … well, it was frightening.

Sometimes you look for God in a waiting room. I prayed to ward off the fear. And I waited, and waited, and waited.

A few hours passed. Suddenly, Dr. Vicken Aharonian, the head of the Kaiser heart cath lab, appeared at the entrance of the waiting room. He was dressed in green scrubs, with a white surgical mask dangling from his ears. He motioned for me to join him in the hallway.

"She's doing fine," he began. "She'll be in the recovery room for about an hour … and then you'll be able to see her. We found something …"

My heart began to race as he continued.

"Your wife has a 95 percent blockage of the ramus artery in her heart …"

"Oh, my God!" I gasped as both fear and hope grabbed me by the throat.

"... and thankfully, it was in a position where we could fix it with a balloon and a stent," Dr. "A" continued. "She is a lucky woman. She should do well."

I nearly collapsed in relief as I shook his hand and offered my thanks.

In the recovery room, Susie was well aware of what had happened. She had been awake through the entire procedure, joking with the nurses, assisting the doctors as they instructed her to move in this direction or that. They even pointed out the blockage to her on a large television monitor in the operating room.

I bent over the bed and kissed her on the cheek.

"I love you," I whispered.

"I love you, too," Susie answered. "I guess we dodged a bullet. I was heading for a heart attack."

I began to sob.

"Thank God. Thank God."

After two days in the hospital, Susie returned home. At our Shabbat table, she said an ancient Jewish prayer, *Birkat ha-Gomel,* recited by those who have survived a danger, returned safely from a long journey, or recovered from a serious illness:

> Praised are You, Lord our God, Sovereign of the universe, who graciously bestows favor upon the undeserving, even as You have bestowed favor upon me.

And, as the ritual specifies, I responded:

> May God who has been gracious to you continue to favor you with all that is good.

The Hope of Goodness

In the first chapter of the Bible, God creates the universe in a most unusual way. Not with earthquakes, not with hurricanes, not with any sort of big bang. No, God creates the world with words.

When God began to create heaven and earth—the earth being
unformed and void, with darkness over the surface of the deep
and a wind from God sweeping over the water—God said, "Let
there be light"; and there was light. God saw that the light was
good, and God separated the light from the darkness. God called
the light Day, and the darkness He called Night. And there was
evening and there was morning, a first day.

Genesis 1:1–5

For each subsequent creation—the earth and seas, vegetation, the lights
in the sky, living creatures in the seas and on land, and human beings—
the Bible proclaims:

Vayar Elohim ki tov—And God saw that this was good.

And, when God's work of creation is completed, the Bible concludes:

Vayar Elohim et kol asher asah v'hinei tov m'od—
And God saw all that God had made and found it very good.

Genesis 1:31

Rabbi Ed Feinstein suggests that *good* is the most important word in this
chapter. "This is the great revolution that began our faith. The whole
world sees chaos, terror, random death as inevitable. And this one little
people, a people who suffered more than any other people, this people
has the cosmic chutzpah (gall) to say 'It doesn't have to be that way!
Come, be God's partner. There is goodness in creating the world.'"

It is remarkable, when you think about it—the stories of hope and
goodness that emerge out of darkness. As a teenager, I remember reading
The Diary of Anne Frank, the chronicles of a Jewish girl hidden away in an
attic in Amsterdam to escape the Nazis, who famously wrote these words:

Despite everything, I believe people are really good at heart.

Anne wrote these words in her diary on July 15, 1944. On August 4, just
three weeks later, Anne and her family, and those in hiding with her, were

discovered and arrested. She and her sister Margot eventually arrived at Bergen-Belsen concentration camp where both contracted typhoid. Anne died of the disease sometime in late December 1944, just three weeks before the Russians liberated the camp.

Although Anne Frank was an eyewitness to the most fearful and evil period of human history, she also knew of the kindness of four employees of her father, Otto, who helped those hidden in the attic for twenty-five months: Miep Gies, Johannes Kleiman, Victor Kugler, and Bep Voskuijl. At great risk of their own lives, they arranged the food supplies, clothing, books, and all sorts of other necessities. These "righteous Gentiles" were evidence of the goodness Anne saw amid the chaos.

What makes someone hopeful? Viktor Frankl, a psychologist and a survivor of Auschwitz, writes in his masterpiece *Man's Search for Meaning*:

> The last and greatest human freedom is the freedom to choose your attitude.

The Hope of God

After Susie's illness, her friends called to inquire about her recovery. They expressed concern that she had narrowly avoided a heart attack and hoped that she was on the right track healthwise. I often responded, "Oh, she's focused now; she has the fear of God in her."

One day, as these words escaped my lips, I caught myself.

"Actually, she doesn't have the *fear* of God in her; she has the *hope* of God."

Have you heard this expression—the fear of God?

The colloquial meaning refers to someone who is terrified, as in: "The doctor put the fear of God into the patient when she told her to lose weight or risk long-term illness."

While the *fear of God* might be motivating, it might just as easily be paralyzing. The term itself is based on a mistranslation of the biblical Hebrew term *yirah* as "fear" when its true meaning is "awe."

The great twentieth-century philosopher Abraham Joshua Heschel often began his evening lectures with this simple statement:

> "Ladies and gentlemen, a great miracle just happened."

Gasps could be heard throughout the audience, the curiosity palpable. What "great miracle" had just occurred? Heschel would pause for effect, and then say:

"The sun just set."

Heschel had grabbed his audience with a striking example of his theme: The everyday occurrences in God's creation are miraculous. But we human beings who see the sun rise and set every day have become accustomed to the regularity; we have lost our sense of awe.

> When we see God as "awe-full," we are inspired to a relationship of hope, not fear. God does not terrify; God inspires. God does not provoke trembling; God offers comfort. God does not scare; God is a vehicle for repair.

For Heschel, awareness of the Divine begins with wonder. He called for an attitude of "radical amazement" toward the world surrounding us. "To see the world through the eyes of wonder is to see God's presence in everything. It was the biblical prophets who elevated the notion of wonder from 'surprised reaction' to a *form of thinking*—an attitude that never ceases." This attitude of wonder leads to *yirah*—awe.

Perhaps nothing illustrates the concept of awe better than nature itself. Rabbi Mike Comins, in his delightful book *A Wild Faith: Jewish Ways into Wilderness, Wilderness Ways into Judaism* (Jewish Lights), argues that the word *yirah* probably did mean "fear" originally, because *fear* and *awe* are inextricably related:

> The two meanings are connected. The paradigmatically awesome moments of life, such as childbirth, are filled with danger. The mystery, fragility, and preciousness of our existence pervades awe-filled moments. The difference is that when we feel fear, say as in a lightning storm, we want to run. When we feel awe, we want to stick around. We are attracted.
>
> *A Wild Faith*, page 23

According to Heschel, awe precedes faith ... it is at the root of faith. We must grow in awe in order to reach faith. We must be guided by awe to be worthy of faith. Awe rather than faith is the cardinal attitude of the religious Jew.

When we see God as "awe-full," we are inspired to a relationship of hope, not fear. God does not terrify; God inspires. God does not provoke trembling; God offers comfort. God does not scare; God is a vehicle for repair.

When times are tough, let the hope of God lead you to a time of goodness, health, and blessing.

The Only Thing to Fear

Hope is the thing with feathers
That perches in the soul,
And sings the tune—without the words,
And never stops at all.

And sweetest in the gale is heard;
And sore must be the storm
That could abash the little bird
That kept so many warm.

I've heard it in the chillest land,
And on the strangest sea;
Yet, never, in extremity,
It asked a crumb of me.

Emily Dickinson

I write these words during tough times. The worldwide economy is in the midst of a severe recession. The subprime credit debacle has led to millions of foreclosed homes, a withering of stock portfolios, and a loss of confidence in the markets. Millions of workers are losing their jobs. Whole industries are in danger of declaring bankruptcy. The prognosis is dire: Things are likely to get worse before they get better. The people are afraid.

Some observers liken these days to those during the Great Depression of the 1930s when one-quarter of America's banks folded and millions stood in breadlines. The people were afraid then as well.

It took a visionary president to rally the country with a call to action. Franklin Delano Roosevelt, in his famous First Inaugural Address to the nation on March 4, 1933, uttered these stirring words:

> This is preeminently the time to speak the truth, the whole truth, frankly and boldly. Nor need we shrink from honestly facing conditions in our country today. This great nation will endure, as it has endured, will revive and will prosper.
>
> So, first of all, let me assert my firm belief that the only thing we have to fear is fear itself—nameless, unreasoning, unjustified terror, which paralyzes needed efforts to convert retreat into advance. In every dark hour of our national life, a leadership of frankness and of vigor has met with that understanding and support of the people themselves, which is essential to victory. And I am convinced that you will again give that support to leadership in these critical days.... Happiness lies not in the mere possession of money; it lies in the joy of achievement, in the thrill of creative effort. The joy, the moral stimulation of work no longer must be forgotten in the mad chase of evanescent profits. These dark days, my friends, will be worth all they cost us if they teach us that our true destiny is not to be ministered unto but to minister to ourselves, to our fellow men.

President Roosevelt put millions of workers on the front lines of projects to build the infrastructure of America, tightened controls on financial institutions, and inspired thousands to enter public service. The country responded to his call to overcome fear through a combination of hope and action. Within months, a new attitude buoyed the people.

The Audacity of Hope

A student of history, President Barack Obama understands the power of hope. His manifesto outlining the reasons he ran for the presidency is titled

The Audacity of Hope. He reflects on the people he met on the campaign trail to be U.S. senator from Illinois as he prepares for the speech to the 2004 Democratic National Convention that catapulted him to national attention:

> I remembered Tim Wheeler and his wife in Galesburg, trying to figure out how to get their teenage son the liver transplant he needed. I remembered a young man in East Moline named Seamus Ahern who was on his way to Iraq—the desire he had to serve his country, the look of pride and apprehension on the face of his father. I remembered a young black woman in East St. Louis whose name I never did catch, but who told me of her efforts to attend college even though no one in her family had ever graduated from high school.
>
> It wasn't just the struggles of these men and women that moved me. Rather, it was their determination, their self-reliance, a relentless optimism in the face of hardship....
>
> The audacity of hope.
>
> That was the best of the American spirit, I thought—having the audacity to believe despite all the evidence to the contrary that we could restore a sense of community to a nation torn by conflict; the gall to believe that despite personal setbacks—the loss of a job or an illness in the family or a childhood mired in poverty, we had some control—and therefore responsibility—over our own fate.
>
> It was that audacity, I thought, that joined us as one people. It was that pervasive spirit of hope that tied my own family's story to the larger American story, and my own story to those of the voters I sought to represent.
>
> *The Audacity of Hope*, pages 356–357

Both presidents understood that their greatest challenge was to overcome the paralyzing effects of fear by giving people hope. Both men did so by telling the truth about the situation, not by refusing to face the grim realities of their time. They appealed to the resilience of the American spirit, the ethic of hard work, and the call to service. There was no escaping the need for sacrifice, no avoiding the belt-tightening and delayed gratification that would be required. Yet the combination of transparency, innovative ideas for putting the country back to work, and renewed regulatory control moved the country forward, creating a climate of confidence that better days were ahead.

Hatikvah—The Hope

In another part of the world at a different time, a song captured this spirit of national hope. When one of the first modern Jewish settlements, Petach Tikvah, was established in Palestine, Naftali Hertz Imber, a Ukrainian Jew, put into words the two-thousand-year-old dream of the Jewish people to return from exile and establish the modern State of Israel. Originally published as a nine-stanza poem, *Tikvateinu* ("Our Hope"), the piece was adopted as the anthem of the Zionist movement at the First Zionist Congress in 1897. Set to a folk melody by Samuel Cohen, an immigrant from Moldavia, the original words were adapted over the years into the anthem known as *Hatikvah* ("The Hope").

On May 16, 1948, the State of Israel was established, and Jews across the world sang *Hatikvah* with joy in their hearts and tears in their eyes. A two-thousand-year-old hope that had sustained a people was finally realized.

As long as in the heart within,	*Kol 'od baleivav penimah*
A Jewish soul still yearns,	*Nefesh yehudi homiyah*
And onward toward the ends of the east	*Ul(e)fa'atei mizrach kadimah*
An eye still gazes toward Zion.	*Ayin letziyon tzofiya.*
Our hope will not be lost,	*Od lo avdah tikvateinu*
The hope of two thousand years—	*Hatikvah bat shnot alpayim*
To be a free people in our land,	*Lihyot 'am chofshi be'artzeinu*
The land of Zion and Jerusalem.	*Eretz tzion v'Yerushalayim.*

Hope Is a Gift

I will never forget the phone call. It was my mother ... and she was weeping.

"Ronnie, you'll never believe it," she cried. "Billy Rosen has cancer."

The words felt like a stake through my heart. The closest first cousin to me in age, Billy and I had grown up together, gone to school together, and shared family together. He was fifty-six years old. Two years earlier, his beloved brother, Paul, had succumbed to pancreatic cancer at the age of fifty-five.

"Oh, my God!" I exclaimed. "Aunt Rose must be devastated." I could not imagine how my mother's sister would handle this latest challenge in her life, having lost both her husband and her elder son to cancer ... and now this.

I picked up the phone to call Bill. Always thoughtful and intelligent, Bill measured his words carefully.

"I'm prepared to fight this, Ronnie," he said. "I begin chemotherapy immediately. I plan to make it to Daniel and Kate's wedding. I will fight for my life ... and hope for the best."

Hope for the best. How can hope help fight cancer?

According to Jessie Gruman, a cancer survivor and the author of *AfterShock: What to Do When the Doctor Gives You—Or Someone You Love—a Devastating Diagnosis,* there are six ways to help someone who has cancer:

1. Acknowledge the situation
2. Offer help only if you can deliver
3. Guard our privacy
4. Listen to us
5. Remember that hope is a gift
6. Ensure our dignity

But, Gruman warns, "We don't always feel it. When you insist that we be hopeful and positive, we feel we have failed when we aren't. Don't cut off the possibility that we will share our burden with you and the opportunity to support us through hard times."

Bill did fight his cancer. With the incredible support of his wife, Margo, his adult children, Daniel and David, and his family, Bill made it to Kate and Daniel's beautiful wedding. Knowing full well that his days were numbered, Bill took every opportunity to spend time with his loved ones. He rented a house in the Caribbean so the family could enjoy an escape from the winter in Omaha. He traveled to the West Coast to see old college friends and family. He made trips to Chicago and New York to enjoy theater and museums. He acquired lovely antiques for his collection. Bill's hope and will to live enabled him to survive two years longer than the doctor's prognosis.

In the end, Bill insisted on leaving the hospital and returning to his home, where Margo installed a bed in his den. There, surrounded by his cherished books, soothed by the classical music he loved, and attended to day and night by his family and friends, Bill faced his last days with courage and dignity.

I was asked to deliver the eulogy. Standing before a large gathering of his community, I recalled Bill's life and reflected on his legacy.

Bill Rosen was a fine man.

He filled his life with everything fine:

Fine literature, fine wine, fine food, fine movies, fine furnishings, fine journeys, fine music, fine friends …

I have known Billy, as I affectionately called him, literally my entire life. We were born in the same year, attended the same junior high school, studied French from Bev Fellman—Billy loved one of her slide shows because it began: "Margo, Margo! *Fait ses valises!*" We worked on the Central High newspaper together and have children the same ages. He met Margo Neesman in the seventh grade and they became fast friends. Steve Neesman recalls that Bill was over to the house so often, he considered him his older brother. In college, they realized that you could fall in love with your best friend … and that's what happened. A thirty-five-year marriage of best friends.

Their proudest achievement and Bill's lasting legacy is, of course, two magnificent sons. Just as Uncle Ben and Aunt Rose raised two wonderful boys, so did Bill and Margo. Yesterday, Margo showed me a book that Bill just loved to read, a collection of Jewish humor. I looked through it and Bill had put a post-it note next to one of the stories. It goes like this:

A Jewish mother is walking down the street with her two young sons.

A passerby asks her: "How old are your boys?"

She replies: "The doctor is four, and the lawyer is two."

Bill was so proud of Daniel and David, the best doctor and lawyer in the United States of America. And he welcomed Kate in the family as the daughter he always hoped for.... These are young people of remarkable achievement: Bill loved to tell everyone that Daniel was working at a Harvard-affiliated hospital ... and David rejected Harvard to attend NYU Law School to pursue his passion for social justice.

The three of you are Bill's immortality. He was a great teacher—not simply with his words, but with the very way he lived. You have learned his life lessons well.

You have learned the art of patience—to slow down and appreciate the beauty in everything from a fine story to a fine breeze on a summer's afternoon.

You have learned how to love—you have been eyewitness to how much your father loved his father, his mother, his brother, his family, his friends; and, most of all, his love for the love of his life—Margo ... and his love for you. You all know how much he loved you.

And, your dad taught you how to live life—not just in the good times—that's easy. You have learned how to live through illness, through struggle, and through loss.

It is said that we die as we live. Bill Rosen lived a life of dignity, even through incredible pain. He never complained about the pain ... he only apologized for it. "I'm sorry," he'd say, "I just can't move right now." He never worried about himself; he only worried about everyone else: his mom, his kids, his wife—who has been tireless in her devotion to his care. Two days ago, when he managed to awake for a few seconds, he opened his eyes, looked up at Margo, and said: "How are you?" They were his last words.

> God as Deliverer shows that God is a God concerned with the ongoing story of humankind, a God who cares, a God who inspires us to be God's partner in the ongoing creation and repair of the world.

We will need this wisdom in the days ahead ... for there is no denying that we are in the midst of a terrible loss ... an unspeakable loss for his mother, for his wife and children, for all of us.

How can we be but bereaved? How can we be but blue?

And yet, through our grief, let us remember the great blessings this elegant man brought to us. Let us hold him in our hearts forever. Let us kiss him good-bye, let us bring him to his Eternal Rest, let us comfort each other as he would comfort us. Let us be grateful that our lives were touched by this wonderful, wonderful ... this fine, fine soul.

Zichrono livracha—may his memory always be a blessing.

We love you, Billy.

A Life Half-Lived

In the wonderful 1992 film *Strictly Ballroom,* director Baz Luhrmann offers a meditation on the paralyzing power of fear and the catalyzing power of hope. Set in the topsy-turvy world of Australian ballroom dancing, all the central characters live in fear: fear of losing, fear of breaking rules, fear of change, fear of loving, fear of dancing. Only a beginner dancer, Fran— an ugly duckling immigrant from Spain—has the courage to overcome her fears to fulfill her dreams. When her reluctant dance partner, Scott, begins to question his decision to dance "new steps" with a rank amateur, she offers him an old Spanish proverb to reassure him:

> To live a life in fear will stifle, suffocate, and strangle your creativity, your drive, your enthusiasm.

Vivir con miedo, es como vivir a medias!—A life lived in fear is a life half lived!

According to the dictionary, *fear* is a painful emotion or passion excited by the expectation of evil, or the apprehension of impending danger. Fear stops us from trying new steps, attempting different experiences, working toward our dreams. A life lived in fear limits us; a life lived in hope empowers us.

A popular Hebrew song, based on the teaching of Rebbe Nachman of Breslov, offers a similar message:

> *Kol ha-olam kulo gesher tzar m'od.*
> *Ve'ha-ikar lo l'fachaid klal.*
> The whole world is like a narrow bridge.

But the most essential thing is this:
Do not fear.

This is what our Fourth Question we're asked in heaven asks of us:
Tzipita li'yeshuah? Did you hope for deliverance?
Was your life lived in hope?
And if it was, what did you hope for?

Hope for Deliverance

The term *li'yeshuah* may be translated as "deliverance," "redemption," or "salvation."

The word *salvation* is laden with Christian meaning, even though it originated as a Jewish value. In Christianity, it means "being saved," as it describes the process of an individual becoming absolved of sins through a belief in Jesus as the Messiah. The Jewish concept of *li'yeshuah* refers to God's deliverance of the Jewish people, a communal "saving" from harm. For example, the Passover seder is a ritual commemorating the—pick your preferred term—*deliverance, redemption,* or *salvation* of the Israelites from slavery in Egypt.

There are, however, liturgical formulations that speak of a personal relationship between human beings and God the Deliverer. Consider the opening paragraph of the Havdalah ceremony, marking the separation between the sacred time of Shabbat and the regular time of the workweek. The prayer is a series of biblical texts about *yeshuah:*

> *Hinei, El yishu'ati evtach velo efchad, ki azi vezimrat Yah, Adonai, va'yehi li li'yeshuah.*
> Behold, God is my Deliverer, I will trust God and not be afraid, for my strong faith and song of praise for God will be my deliverance.
> > Isaiah 12:2

> *U'she'avtem ma'yim besason, mima'a'yenay ha'yeshuah.*
> You will draw water joyously from the wells of deliverance.
> > Isaiah 12:3

La'Adonai ha'yeshuah, al amcha virchatecha, Selah.
Deliverance is God's; may Your blessing rest upon Your people,
Selah.

Psalms 3:9

Adonai Tzeva'ot imanu, misgav lanu, Elohay Ya'akov, Selah.
God of the heavenly armies is with us; the Lord of Jacob is a
fortress protecting us, *Selah.*

Psalms 46:12

Adonai Tzeva'ot, ashray adam botay'ach bach.
God of the heavenly armies, happy is the individual who trusts
You.

Psalms 84:13

Adonai hoshi'ah, ha-melech ya'anaynu ve'yom kor'aynu.
God, deliver us! The Sovereign will answer us on the day we
call upon God.

Psalms 20:10

La'yehudim ha'yetah orah vesimcha vesason vikar;
The Jews had light, happiness, joy and honor;
kayn te'hi'yeh lanu.
may we have the same.

Esther 8:16

Kos yeshu'ot esa u'veshaym Adonai ekra.
I will raise the cup of deliverance and call out in the name of
God.

Psalms 116:13

As the Sabbath ends, the theme is hope—hope that God will watch over,
answer, and deliver the people to a week of joy, happiness, light, and honor.

The Havdalah service concludes with the singing of "*Eliyahu Ha-Navi,*"
a song of hope that Elijah the prophet, harbinger of the messianic time,
will come "speedily in our day."

Passover and Hope

These two themes—being unafraid of the "narrow bridge" and "hope for deliverance"—come together in the holiday of Passover. The purpose of the Passover seder is to relive the Exodus from *Mitzrayim*, the "narrow" (*zar*) place, the place of slavery and oppression, pessimism and despair.

I never quite got this message at my grandfather's seder table. Zadie Louie was a grocer, so we used the Maxwell House Haggadah, of course. There is one good thing about the Maxwell House Haggadah—it's free! Think of it. As far as I know, this is the only holy text with ads in the back. One day hundreds of years from now, archeologists will excavate Jewish homes in North America to try to understand how Jews lived in the twentieth century and they will find a Maxwell House Haggadah ... with ads for coffee on the back cover. Imagine if Yigal Yadin, the famous Israeli archeologist, had discovered the Dead Sea Scrolls, unrolled the text, and on the last parchment he found an advertisement for "Shlomo's Dates."

The true hero of the Passover seder is, of course, God. Moses is hardly mentioned in the story. How can that be? It's as if someone telling the story of the founding of America never spoke about George Washington. God is the Deliverer of the Israelite slaves from the house of bondage, not Moses. It is God who is deserving of praise in section after section of the Haggadah.

God liberates the people from Egypt and they wander in the Sinai desert for forty years. There they receive the Ten Commandments. Curiously, the First Commandment does not refer to God as the Creator of the heavens and the earth. Rather, God addresses the people with this definition:

> The question I will be asked in heaven is this:
>
> "Did you betray who you were ... or did you do what you hoped?"
>
> My prayer for myself is: "Did I listen to the voice of my own soul?"
>
> Or, maybe God will ask about my life on earth:
>
> "How was it?"
>
> NESHAMA CARLEBACH

I am the Lord your God who brought you out of the land of
Egypt, the house of bondage. You shall have no other gods
besides Me.

Exodus 20:2

The commentators ask: Why is the emphasis on God as Redeemer and not
God as Creator? God could have created the world and let whatever happens happen. But God as Deliverer shows that God is a God concerned
with the ongoing story of humankind, a God who cares, a God who
inspires us to be God's partner in the ongoing creation and repair of the
world. This is a personal God, a God who searches for human beings,
who needs us as much as we need God.

The "narrow" place of Egypt can be thought of as a metaphor for any
"house of bondage," any enslavement, any personal challenge. Are there
not times when we feel like "crying out" to God to be saved from a problem, an affliction, an addiction that narrows us?

The most powerful sentence in the Passover Haggadah makes this clear:

In every generation, all of us should consider ourselves as if we
were brought out from Egypt.

The seder is not just a history lesson. This is a celebration rooted in the
"hope for deliverance" today. It is why we sing the *Hallel*, praising God the
Deliverer. It is why we sing "*Eliyahu Ha-Navi,*" opening the door as a symbolic gesture of our hope for messianic times.

Choose Hope

When you think about it, the Fourth Question you're asked in heaven is
about your *attitude*. The first three questions ask about what you *did*—did
you act with honesty, did you learn from everyone, did you leave a legacy?
This question is about how you *felt*.

Were you a hopeful optimist or a fearful pessimist?

It is easy to succumb to the pessimist's view of the world. The glass is
half-empty. Politicians are corruptible. You can't trust anyone. Bad people
get away with murder.

But to live a life in fear will stifle, suffocate, and strangle your creativity, your drive, your enthusiasm.

When you get to heaven, you will be asked: Did you have hope in your heart?

Did you see the glass as half-full? Did you hear the call for a new kind of politics? Did you believe that the sun would come out tomorrow? Did you control your fears and walk across the narrow bridge?

Choose hope.

Keep hope alive.

It will serve you well ... during your life well lived.

On the next page, I invite you to reflect on your answers to the Fourth Question you're asked in heaven.

How do you have hope in your heart?

5

What Matters Most

Do you know what grout is?

I had no idea.

I thought it had something to do with your feet.

But when Susie one day said to me as she looked at the tiles on our kitchen counter, "Ronnie, we need some grout," I was soon on my way to the local Home Depot and not the doctor's office.

I must admit that I am not much of a fix-things-around-the-house kind of guy. So walking into the Home Depot was a bit intimidating. It was a busy place—contractors, painters, handymen walking in purposefully, heading for the materials they needed. I, on the other hand, kind of sauntered in sheepishly, hoping I wouldn't be too embarrassed over my lack of knowledge.

I was warmly greeted by the first person in an orange apron I met. Among the many buttons and decals on the apron was one that said: "Ask me." So I asked.

"Can you help me with grout?"

"Certainly," Mark replied. (His name, "Mark," was written in black magic marker on the apron.) "What's your name?"

"Ron. Thanks," I said, as we began walking through the cavernous store.

I suppose Mark picked up on my nervous vibe because as we approached the grout section, he asked, "Ever work with grout before, Ron?"

"No, not really. To tell you the truth, I thought it had something to do with your feet."

Mark laughed knowingly.

"Ah, don't worry. I'll show you what to do," he reassured me.

When we arrived at the aisle, I saw dozens of tubes and packages labeled *grout*.

Mark picked up a brand-new tube and said, "Follow me!"

We walked over to a worktable. Mark reached underneath and pulled out several tiles. He opened the tube and started to explain, "Look, Ron, grout is a kind of paste that's used to cement tiles in place. It's that stuff you see between the tiles in your shower or on a countertop." With that, Mark began applying the grout between two of the demonstration tiles.

"How much do you need to use?" I asked.

"Good question, Ron," Mark replied. "It depends on the thickness of the tile. You sort of judge it as you do it. You can always remove excess grout with a little tool we call a grout float. Here, let me show you."

Mark walked back to the aisle to pick up a brand-new grout float, opened the package, and smoothed out the grout with the tool.

"Do I put the new grout over the old grout?" I wondered.

"Good question, Ron. If you have old grout that you need to remove, you'll want a grout scraper," Mark explained as he grabbed one off the shelf.

At this point, I had begun to relax and the questions came flowing.

"How long does it take to dry? Does it come in different colors? What if I get it all over my hands? Is there grout soap?"

Mark considered and answered each and every question with respect. Then, after demonstrating how to grout tile, he produced two more tiles and invited me to try it. With a gentle suggestion or two, I managed to get the grout between the tiles successfully, smoothing the line out with the float.

"See," Mark smiled. "Nothing to it, Ron! You'll do fine. Here, let's get what you need."

Escorting me back to the grout section, Mark grabbed a basket and began loading it with all the supplies I needed to do the job. As he did, I began to hum the ubiquitous Home Depot jingle. Mark got a kick out of that.

"Hey," I smiled. "I can do it. You just helped!"

I left the Home Depot that morning equipped and empowered to do the work at home. And never once in the entire interaction with Mark did I feel like I was asking a stupid question.

Perhaps it was Mark's welcoming attitude. Or his willingness to use brand new products. Or his expert demonstration of how to do the task.

But I think it was his acceptance and validation of my queries. "Good question, Ron."

He recognized that I was a novice, that I was nervous about tackling the task. Mark had created a safe atmosphere for me to learn a new skill. And he had done so not only by allowing but also by welcoming my questions.

How to Study

Our teacher, Rava, imagines that the Fifth Question you'll be asked in heaven will be a two-parter:

1. *Pilpalta b'chochmah?*
2. *Havanta davar mitoch davar?*

Shabbat 31a

The simple meaning of the words is this:

1. Did you seek wisdom?
2. Did you understand one thing from another?

On the surface, these questions appear to be about how one studies and learns. Recall that Rava is a Rabbi of the Talmud. He has already asked the Third Question you'll be asked in heaven: "Did you set a time for Torah?" Clearly, study—the act of learning—is an important task for navigating life on earth. But *how* do you study? What is the best *way* to study?

The methodology of "studying" is an age-old concern. Think of the Socratic Method you probably learned in high school. Named after the famous Greek philosopher, Socrates, the Socratic Method instructs the questioner to explore the implications of another's positions, to stimulate rational thinking and illuminate ideas. Sometimes called the "dialectical method," the learning comes from an oppositional discussion in which one point of view is pitted against another.

As we've learned, in classic Jewish study of Talmud called *chevrutah* (from *chaver,* meaning "friend"), two students sit opposite each other with a text in between them and discuss the meaning of the verses by asking questions. The questions are designed to analyze the arguments advanced by the Rabbis of the Talmud. Often, this manner of study results in the two "friends" engaging in heated dialectical discussions. But, in the end, the rigorous process yields a deeper learning, a learning that encompasses all sides of an argument.

> Did you figure out what was really important?
>
> NAN ZAITLEN

In fact, in both talmudic and Socratic methods, the real value of the study comes from debating and understanding opposite points of view. After the arguments have been presented, a decision is made as to what the law should be. But all the arguments are included in the record— even the minority opinions. In the Talmud, all arguments are duly recorded. In American jurisprudence as well—even in the Supreme Court of the land—both the majority and the minority opinions are respected.

The apparent intent of Rava's questions is to ask whether you learned how to study during your life on earth. When I entered college as a freshman at Washington University in St. Louis, I remember well that the first book handed to me was a study skills manual. They wanted me to learn how to study, too. Rava's two questions seem to be a kind of instruction guide for his students as they swim in the sea of Talmud, a lifelong pursuit.

Deeper Questions

I think there is a deeper meaning in Rava's questions.

The clues are in the words he uses.

In the first question, we find the word *chochmah*—wisdom.

In Jewish study, there are three kinds of knowledge: *chochmah, binah,* and *da'at.*

According to my esteemed teacher, Rabbi Elliot Dorff, *chochmah* is the kind of knowledge that one gains from *experience*—wisdom.

In the second question, we find the word *havanta*—understanding.

The root word of *havanta* is *binah. Binah* refers to *analytic* ability—understanding that comes from analyzing arguments and reaching conclusions.

Da'at is factual knowledge: the what, where, when, and how of a "thing"—*davar.*

Put it all together and we come to another way to read Rava's questions:

1. *Pilpalta b'***chochmah***?*
    Did you ask questions about your life experiences that led you to **wisdom**?

2. **Havanta** *davar mitoch davar?*
    Did your analysis lead you to **understanding**?

Now we're not just getting at *how* to study, but *why* we study.

The Purpose of Wisdom and Understanding

Life is full of choices. Every day, seemingly every hour, there are important decisions to be made. Should I sleep in an extra ten minutes and risk running late to work? If I eat fried eggs instead of poached, will my cholesterol go sky high? Is it time to confront my boss about his negative attitude? He could fire me or I might quit. My daughter is performing in the school play this afternoon, but I'm expected at a crucial meeting. Can I miss it? My son wants to attend an Ivy League school where the tuition is three times higher than our fine local state university. Can I afford it? What should I do with my ninety-nine-year-old father-in-law who wants to continue driving a car? It is his last vestige of independence, but I fear that he might hurt himself or others.

I think the purpose of the Fifth Question you're asked in heaven is to help guide you in making decisions. How? By asking questions that lead to wisdom and understanding the implications of your choices.

Dreying

For some people, this business of making decisions is no easy thing.

Permit me to teach you a great Yiddish word.

Dreying.

It comes from the word *drey,* meaning "to spin."

Drey is the root word of *dreydle,* the four-sided spinning top used in a popular Hanukkah game.

In my family, I grew up with another usage of the word: *dreykop*.

A *dreykop* is someone who is always turning, always thinking about her next move.

In his hilarious dictionary, *The Joys of Yiddish,* Leo Rosten defines a *dreykop* as someone who "talks you into something," who "turns your head" or confuses you. He explains:

> The following involves two *dreykops*, as far as I'm concerned.
>
> The phone rang in the law offices. A voice answered: "Zucker, Zucker, Zucker and Zucker."
>
> "Hello, may I please speak to Mr. Zucker?"
>
> "I'm sorry, but Mr. Zucker is in court."
>
> "Well, then, can I speak to Mr. Zucker?"
>
> "Sorry, Mr. Zucker is in Washington."
>
> "Well, how about connecting me with Mr. Zucker?"
>
> "Mr. Zucker won't be in until two."
>
> Sigh. "Okay, then, I'll speak to Mr. Zucker."
>
> "Speaking."

Dreying does not always have a negative connotation. For example, I *drey* all the time. When I am faced with a decision, I weigh options in my mind, envisioning the consequences of each choice I could make, trying to assess the impact of what is likely to happen. I have this GPS system built into my brain that lays out a map of alternative paths. But instead of some lovely woman's voice making the decisions about which way to turn, I get to decide.

Dreying could very possibly be hardwired in the Jewish DNA. It certainly is in mine. My mother, Bernice, is a first-class *dreyer.* In that keen mind of hers, she keeps in play a whole roster of personalities—children, grandchildren, sisters, nieces and nephews, doctors, and friends—curious to know what's going on in their lives, asking penetrating questions about their life stories and plans, and, more often than not, offering her wisdom based on years of experience. Mom loves a project—putting on an elegant fund-raiser for her beloved Nebraska Foundation for Visually Impaired Children, organizing a wedding shower, constantly working the phones to recruit this person or that to get involved in a cause.

My father, Alan, is a pretty good *dreyer,* too. He puts his visioning skills to work as an inventor. I love visiting with him on my trips to Omaha. Within minutes of walking into their apartment, Dad will pull out his latest idea: a device to help you find your car in a parking lot, a new improved way to use dental floss, and he actually did invent and patent a revolutionary toothbrush that brushes both sides of your teeth simultaneously!

My brother, Bob, an accomplished civil servant now working in the senior management of the Anti-Defamation League (ADL) as associate national director of regional operations, is quite the *dreyer.* Extraordinarily intelligent and just as exuberant, Bobby always had difficulty deciding what to do simply because so many things were interesting to him. Once he settled on a career as the regional director of the Plain States Region of the Anti-Defamation League, Bob became a beloved leader in Omaha and the surrounding area, garnering the respect and admiration of community leaders as he fought against prejudice and hate in a distinguished eighteen-year stint, working with school groups, police departments, and government officials.

When Bob accepted the offer to move to New York City to head all the regions of the ADL, the community held a gala farewell banquet in his honor that attracted more than five hundred movers and shakers, including politicians, police chiefs, religious leaders, and philanthropists. The feeling in the ballroom was electric. Everyone was so grateful for Bobby's positive *dreying,* which had led to so many engaging initiatives in the schools, congregations, and halls of government.

The Rabbis of the Talmud were also *dreyers.* They engaged in long discussions to decipher the meaning of biblical texts and ancient laws and customs. They developed sophisticated answers to questions of behavior and ethical conduct. How? Through a unique process they called *pilpul,* the give-and-take of argument, *l'sheim shamayin,* for the sake of heaven. Yes, the ancient Rabbis were, in the nicest sense of the word, *dreykops.*

Putting It All Together

Ultimately, though, we must stop the *dreying.*

The Fifth Question asks:

Were you able to combine your analytical abilities with your hard-won wisdom from experience to make good choices?

Did you live your life making decisions based on these gifts?

Could you distinguish between what was really important and what was not?

Did you learn to *prioritize*?

The Fifth Question you're asked in heaven leads to this:
When you look at your life, did you get your priorities straight?

Prioritizing

The word *prioritize* has an interesting etymology. It begins with the noun *prior,* a twelfth-century title of the superior rank in a monastery; the *prior* was also the superior of a house in various religious communities. By the fourteenth century, the word *priority* referred to a preferential ranking or superiority in rank, position, or privilege. Then, during the tumultuous period between 1965 and 1970, someone coined the term *prioritize,* meaning "to list or rate [projects or goals] in order of priority." In the language of the time, "You gotta prioritize, man!" Among competing alternatives, what is your top *priority*?

Oprah's Priority

Susie is a catalog and magazine junkie. Every day, our mailbox is jammed with piles of these things. She loves to skim them for creative ideas and she shops for unusual items.

I write this on New Year's Eve 2008. This afternoon, I happened to notice a striking cover photo on the January 2009 issue of Susie's copy of *O—The Oprah Magazine*.

I will describe it in a moment.

There is no more powerful woman in television or, for that matter, in popular culture than talk show host Oprah Winfrey. She has created a program that is must-see TV for millions of viewers who follow her every suggestion, whether it be recommendations for reading through Oprah's Book Club or her famous "Oprah's Favorite Things." No doubt, she is one of the most influential communicators in the world.

Over the years, Oprah has waged a very public battle with her weight. She has been svelte … and not. A few years ago, she dazzled the world with a fantastic weight loss brought about through healthy food choices and vigorous exercise. During the past year, she dealt with a thyroid problem and an overextended schedule. She began to gain back the weight she had lost—and she felt terrible. She was prescribed medications, but it made her "feel as if I were viewing life through a veil." Her friend and health coach, Bob Greene, suggested that she might be in some sort of depression.

> **When you look at your life, did you get your priorities straight?**

"Me—depressed?" Oprah wrote in her mea culpa article. Having gained and lost a lot of weight myself over the years, I was curious to read her story. Greene's comment was a wake-up call. She asked her doctors to ease her off the medications. She took some much-needed time off to "allow my body to restore itself." She began to focus on her food choices and returned to a regular workout schedule. And she came to realize that her weight issues were about something far more important than food. Here's how Oprah herself describes the life lessons she learned:

> What I've learned this year is that my weight issue isn't about eating less or working out harder, or even about a malfunctioning thyroid. It's about my life being out of balance, with too much work and not enough play, not enough time to calm down. I let the well run dry…. I don't have a weight problem—I have a self-care problem that manifests itself through weight.
>
> When I stop and ask myself, What am I really hungry for? The answer is always I'm hungry for balance, I'm hungry to do something other than work. If you look at your overscheduled routine and realize, like I did, that you're just going and going and that your work and obligations have become substitutes for life, then you have no one else to blame. Only you can take the reins back.
>
> That's what I'm doing. These days I've put myself back on my own priority list; I try to do at least one hour of exercise five or six days a week. As I work out, eat healthfully, and reorder my life

so there's time to replenish my energy, I continue to do the spiritual and emotional work to conquer this battle once and for all.

And then, as Oprah often does, in a gesture of the sort that endears her to millions, she put a photo of her current 200-pound self in a baggy sweatsuit standing next to a cut-out of her toned 160-pound self in a hip-hugging, bare-midriff, belly-button-showing-off exercise outfit from four years earlier. In her introduction to the New Year's issue, she challenged her readers:

> It's 2009. Do you know where your life is? Well, as this month's cover photo clearly illustrates, we all suffer setbacks from time to time. We allow stress to get the better of us, we put ourselves at the bottom of our own priority list, we sleepwalk through the possibility of joy.

What is on your priority list?
Who is on your priority list?
How do you decide what takes priority?
This is the import of the Fifth Question you're asked in heaven.

The Mom-in-Chief

Michelle Obama has her priorities straight.

Imagine that your husband has just been nominated to be the Democratic candidate for president of the United States of America. You have given a stirring speech about why you think he would be an excellent choice. Walking backstage, your two young daughters, Malia and Sasha, greet you with a request that brings you down to earth: "Mom, we have something important to tell you. We need to have a sleepover!"

According to Michelle Obama, "That snapped me out of speech mode, with the bright lights and applause, and back into the role I love: Mom. The next night, sixteen giggling girls—my daughters, the Biden granddaughters, and friends—took over our hotel room."

A few weeks later, when Barack Obama was elected the forty-fourth president of the United States, Michelle Obama shared her priority list with an eager nation:

Now that Barack has been elected president, it will be an honor to be First Lady. I will work daily on the issues closest to my heart: helping working women and families, particularly military families. But, as my girls reminded me in Denver, even as First Lady, my no. 1 job is still to be Mom. At seven and ten, our daughters are young. My first priority will be to ensure they stay grounded and healthy, with normal childhoods—including home-work, chores, dance, and soccer.

Our girls are the center of Barack's and my world. They're the reason he ran for president—to make the world a better place for them and for all children. For us, and for millions of Americans, that's what this election has been about—making sure that America remains a country where everyone can fulfill their God-given potential…. They are the last thing I think about before falling asleep at night and the first thing on my mind when I wake up in the morning.

What Matters

A priority is what matters most.

The Fifth Question you're asked in heaven leads you to this question: What matters to you?

If you want a clue, think about how you spend your time each day, each week. How much of your time is allocated to work? How much time for your family? How much time for volunteering? How much time for play? How much time for sleep? How much time for eating? How much time for watching television, surfing the Internet, answering your e-mails?

Are the things you spend the most time on the things that matter most?

If not, you may want to combine your analytical abilities with your hard-won wisdom from experience to make better choices.

I know. I know. I am asking you a tough question, an ultimate question about how you choose to live your life, how you choose to use your time, how to create a priority list that reflects your values.

Understanding what matters to you will lead you to a life that matters.

Thirty years ago, Susie and I went together to a weight-loss program that required a daily weigh-in. It drove Susie absolutely crazy. She so feared every morning's confrontation with the scale that she weighed herself nearly every hour, every day.

Now, as anyone who has ever been on a diet knows, your weight fluctuates significantly during the day. For example, you usually weigh less in the morning than you do in the evening. Well, Susie didn't let that get in the way of her hourly trips to the bathroom scale.

As her weight went up during the day, Susie became more and more depressed. She'd get more and more frustrated and angry. Oh, there were times when she lost a tick here and a tick there, and that would restore her enthusiasm. But only until the next visit when, inevitably, the indicator went north.

As I watched her ride this roller coaster of emotions, I became angrier and angrier at the tyranny of the scale. We were living on the third floor of an apartment building at the time. At the end of a particularly bad day of scale-hopping, I finally had had enough.

"If you get on that scale one more time, I'm gonna throw it out!"

> Understanding
> what matters to
> you will lead you to
> a life that matters.

Now it wasn't a very expensive scale. A typical black bathroom model, the kind with a rotating dial that bounced back and forth when you stood on it, until it finally rested on a number. The kind that if you just happened to stand on it with one foot instead of two, your weight loss could be significant.

Well, Susie couldn't help it. She was addicted to getting on that blasted thing at least once an hour. And sure enough, when she came out of the bathroom with tears in her eyes, I flew into action.

I stormed into the bathroom, picked up the scale, and began to walk briskly through the apartment toward the front door.

"What are you doing?" Susie screamed, knowing full well my intentions.

"I'm liberating you from this thing!" I yelled back. "It's driving you crazy and it's driving me crazy. It's history!"

And, with that, I calmly walked down the hall to the trash chute, opened the door, and flung the sucker out!

"Why did you do that?" Susie cried.

"Because I love you. I don't care about the scale. I care about you. That's what matters."

It was the last time we had a scale in our home.

Five Minutes

One way to test your priorities is to think about what would happen if you had only five more minutes to live.

Would you do something?

Would you call someone?

Would you see your life flash before your eyes?

Would you pray?

For me, among the many moving stories that emerged from the terrible tragedy of September 11, 2001, the most haunting and instructive are the accounts of what the doomed people on the upper floors of the World Trade Center did and said as they faced the very real possibility of imminent death.

Melissa Harrington Hughes, thirty-one years old, was attending a conference on the 101st floor of Tower 1. She called her father just nine minutes after the first plane hit.

"She was a little hysterical and I couldn't understand what she was saying so I said, 'Slow down a minute and tell me what the problem is so I can help you out,'" Bob Harrington recalled. "I said, 'You get to the stairwell and get out of that building as fast as you can.' I told her that I loved her. She said, 'I love you too, Dad.' Then she said, 'You have to do me a favor. You have to call Sean and tell him where I am and tell him that I love him.'"

Somehow, Melissa was able to make a second call to her newlywed husband, Sean, sound asleep at 5:56 a.m. in San Francisco. She left a message: "Sean, it's me. I just wanted to let you know I love you and I'm stuck in this building in New York. There's a lot of smoke and I just wanted to let you know that I love you always."

Moises Rivas, a chef at Windows on the World, the renowned restaurant at the top of the center's North Tower, called home as soon as the attack began. He told his stepdaughter, who answered, to tell his wife: "Tell her I'm okay. Tell her I love her, no matter what happens. That's it."

Some people held out hope. Bill Kelly wrote an e-mail message to his sales manager who had written to ask if he was safe. "So far. We're trapped on the 106th floor, but apparently the fire department is almost here."

In those horrific minutes between the collision of the airplanes and the collapse of the towers, others sprang into action.

Michael Benfante, the New York branch manager for the telecom firm Network Plus, was in his office on the 81st floor of Tower 1 when the first plane struck. As the whole building shook, he ordered everyone in his company to evacuate immediately. On the way down, he spotted a woman on the 68th floor in a wheelchair. Since the 1993 bombing of the World Trade Center, special evacuation chairs had been installed to assist the disabled in case of an emergency. Benfante and his colleagues did not hesitate. "We got the woman out of that chair and into the other chair and we started carrying her out," he recalls. "We got to the stairwell and we were carrying her down, sixty-eight stories down the stairs." It took more than an hour to get to the ground floor.

And then, of course, there is the heroic action of a group of passengers on United Airlines Flight 93, hijacked by four terrorists who intended to crash it into either the Capitol or the White House in Washington, D.C. Whether or not one of them yelled *"Let's roll!"* is immaterial. What matters is that they had learned about the attacks on the World Trade Center and the Pentagon and they were determined to prevent another catastrophe. The plane went down in a field outside of Stoneycreek Township in Somerset County, Pennsylvania. The passengers sacrificed themselves to save others.

One Day Before You Die

There is a remarkable teaching in Pirke Avot:

> Rabbi Eliezer taught …
> *Shuv yom echad lifnei mitatach.*
> Repent one day before you die.
>
> Pirke Avot 2:15

Excellent idea.

Only one small problem. How do you know exactly when you will die?

The students posed this dilemma to their teacher, Rabbi Eliezer. The Rabbi answered:

Kol shekein she-ya'aseh teshuvah ha-yom shemah yamut l'machar.
A person should repent every day, lest he die tomorrow.

Avot d'Rabbi Natan, Chapter 15

Repent is one of those difficult words to decipher. It, too, has taken on Christian overtones; *repent* is to ask forgiveness for your "sins."

Another understanding is based on the real meaning of the Hebrew root word *shuv*—"return." It is the core of the term *teshuvah,* often translated as "repentance," but it, too, means "return." Return from what? Return from going astray, return from "missing the mark," the deeper meaning of the Hebrew *chet*—"sin." Think of an archery range. The archer sets an arrow in the bow, lines it up, and lets it go, hoping to hit the bull's-eye. Occasionally, everything is perfect and the arrow pierces the center of the target. More often than not, the archer "misses the mark." The archer tries again, this time adjusting technique, straightening the aim.

Rabbi Eliezer is reminding his students—and us—of an obvious, but no less shattering fact.

You may not get up in the morning.

You may, God forbid, be hit by a drunk driver on the way to the mall this afternoon. That's why you should never go to bed angry with your spouse, your partner, your children.

Never.

That's why you should always kiss them good-night.

Always.

That's why you should ask for forgiveness—and offer forgiveness to those who ask for it.

Immediately.

That's why, in the frantic few minutes of that beautiful September 11 morning, the victims called their spouses, partners, and children to say "I love you" one last time. Because you never know when it will be the last time. So treat every opportunity to reassure, to comfort, as if it were.

One of the great Rabbis, Yochanan ben Zakkai, tells a story in the Talmud that captures the importance of not waiting to make things right.

A king invited his servants to a grand feast, but did not inform them when the feast would be held. The wise ones prepared themselves by dressing in their finest clothes and waiting outside the palace entrance, saying, "Is anything lacking in a royal palace?" The foolish ones, thinking they had plenty of time, ignored the invitation and went back to work, saying, "Can there be a banquet without preparations?" Suddenly, the king asked for all to attend. The wise ones entered dressed appropriately; the foolish ones entered in dirty clothes.... The king invited only the wise servants to sit, eat, drink, and enjoy.

Shabbat 153a

Ask the right questions.
Now.
Be prepared.
Don't wait.

The Last Lecture

My friend Michael Brooks, the exceptionally creative executive director of the University of Michigan Hillel, envisioned an amazing program in 1991 based on Rabbi Eliezer's teaching. Enlisting a group of Michigan students from all parts of the university into an organization called SHOUT—Students Honoring Outstanding University Teaching—a campus-wide election was held to select the UM professor whose "last lecture" they would most want to hear. The professor receives the Golden Apple Award (Michael secured the early sponsorship of Apple Computers), a $1,000 prize, and the opportunity to deliver her or his "last lecture." The annual Golden Apple lecture attracts a standing-room-only crowd of students and staff, an eagerly anticipated event in the UM calendar. Dozens of universities across the nation now emulate the program, including one that has become quite famous, indeed.

In the fall of 2007, Carnegie Mellon University offered a series of lectures in this genre called "Journeys." The first faculty member scheduled to speak was Dr. Randy Pausch, a popular professor of computer science. Shortly before the lecture, Dr. Pausch was diagnosed with terminal pancreatic cancer and given just a few months to live. Opening the talk with his obvious good humor and wit despite his dire prognosis, Pausch told the large gathering of students and faculty: "It's wonderful to be here. What [the organizer] didn't tell you is that this lecture series used to be called the Last Lecture. If you had one last lecture to give before you died, what would it be? I thought, damn, I finally nailed the venue and they renamed it."

> ## Did you love?
> ---
> HOPE LEVY

Then, in a remarkable—and very funny—speech, complete with slides, props, and a birthday cake, Pausch told the journey of his life. He described how he worked to realize his childhood dreams, including defying gravity, playing in the National Football League (not quite), working as a Disney Imagineer, winning the big stuffed animals at an amusement park, and meeting Captain Kirk from *Star Trek*. He then skillfully recounted the even greater thrill of "enabling the dreams of others," mainly by teaching. And finally, he listed his lessons learned:

> Honor and learn from parents, mentors, and students.
>
> Brick walls are there to separate us from the people who don't really want to achieve their dreams.
>
> Don't bail—get a feedback loop and listen to it.
>
> Show gratitude.
>
> Don't complain.
>
> Get good at something—it makes you valuable.
>
> Work hard.
>
> Find the best in everybody.
>
> Be prepared—luck truly is where preparation meets opportunity.

And, then he concluded his "last lecture":

> So today's talk was about my childhood dreams, enabling the
> dreams of others, and some lessons learned. But did you figure
> out the head fake? It's not about how to achieve your dreams. It's
> about how to lead your life. If you lead your life the right way,
> the karma will take care of itself. The dreams will come to you.
> Have you figured out the second head fake? The talk's not for
> you; it's for my kids. Thank you all. Good-night.

Preparing Answers to the Questions

This opportunity—to reflect on your life—does not have to wait for a terminal diagnosis.

You can prepare answers to the Seven Questions you're asked in heaven
all the time.

But there is "prime time."

In the Jewish calendar, the prime time for *teshuvah* is the High Holy Day
period, the ten Days of Return and Renewal between Rosh Hashanah,
the birthday of the world, and Yom Kippur, the Day of Atonement.

> It's not about how
> to achieve your
> dreams. It's about
> how to lead your
> life. If you lead
> your life the right
> way, the karma will
> take care of itself.
> The dreams will
> come to you.

Unfortunately, many Jews enter these ten days
without preparation. Oh, they get dressed nicely
and show up at the synagogue. But they are not
prepared spiritually for the liturgy and the mes-
sages of the holiday.

This is not a new problem. The Rabbis knew
this. So they adjusted the prayers and rituals of
the daily service during the month immediately
preceding the New Year, the month of Elul.
Prayers of repentance are foreshadowed. The
shofar, the piercing call of the ram's horn, is
sounded every morning.

Rabbi Shmuel Herzfeld teaches that the Rabbis
interpret the Hebrew letters spelling Elul—*aleph, lamed, vav,* and *lamed*—to
stand for the well-known verse from Song of Songs: "*Ani l'dodi, v'dodi li—*

I am my beloved's and my beloved is mine." You may have heard the verse at a Jewish wedding; it is a popular vow among young couples. But in the Song of Songs, the imagery of lovers refers to the relationship between God and the people Israel.

God loves you.

Will you love God?

Will you develop a two-way relationship with God during your life on earth, before you get to heaven?

And what if you have doubts about God?

Don't forget that the name *Yisra-El* means "the one who wrestles with God." Just as Jacob wrestled with God, so can you. Who hasn't wrestled with God? The wrestling itself requires relationship—*bein Adam l'Makom*—between human beings and God.

Have the courage to face the fact that you will die.

Everyone does.

We just don't know when.

So prepare yourself.

Return. Again. And again.

Get your priorities straight.

While you still have time.

On the next page, I invite you to reflect on your answers to the Fifth Question you're asked in heaven.

What are your most important priorities?

6

Living to Do

In his marvelous book *Jewish Wisdom*, my friend Rabbi Joseph Telushkin quotes a wonderful story told by Martin Gordon that beautifully illustrates the Sixth Question you're asked in heaven:

> The great leader of nineteenth-century German Orthodoxy, Samson Raphael Hirsch, surprised his disciples one day when he insisted on traveling to Switzerland. "When I stand shortly before the Almighty," he explained, "I will be answerable to many questions.... But what will I say when ... and I'm sure to be asked: 'Why didn't you see my Alps?'"
>
> *Jewish Wisdom*, page 230

I recalled this story while watching the popular 2007 film *The Bucket List*. The movie tells the tale of two men diagnosed with terminal illnesses who decide to create a list of things they want to do or see before they "kick the bucket" and die. Their list:

1. Witness something truly majestic
2. Help a complete stranger for a common good
3. Laugh till I cry
4. Drive a Shelby Mustang
5. Kiss the most beautiful girl in the world
6. Get a tattoo
7. Go skydiving

   8. Visit Stonehenge
   9. Spend a week at the Louvre
  10. See Rome
  11. See the Pyramids
  12. Get back in touch

So off they go skydiving, traveling, driving race cars, and mountain climbing. Along the way, the two men become good friends, sharing their stories and discovering the meaning and purpose of life. The film begins and ends on a "truly majestic" mountain, which, of course, reminded me of Rabbi Hirsch and his desire to see God's Alps before he died.

Have *you* seen God's Alps?

Did you enjoy every magnificent part of God's creation?

In the Jerusalem Talmud, Rabbi Chizkiyah quoted Rabbi Kohen in the name of Rav:

> A human being will have to give account for all that his eye
> beheld and he did not eat.
>
> Kiddushin 4:12

What does this mean?

It means that the Sixth Question you're asked in heaven is not about what you did, but about what you did not do.

The Sixth Question you're asked in heaven asks:

Were there earthly pleasures permitted to you that you did not enjoy?

The Sixth Question asks that we evaluate our time on earth not by how much we learned, not by how badly we messed up, not by how often we prayed—but by how much we loved and enjoyed the world around us.

This is what Rabbi Hirsch understood. As he approached the end of his life, he feared facing his Maker, who stood ready with a searing, penetrating question, "Did you see my Alps?"

The Garden

This notion of enjoying the world is first expressed in the biblical story of *gan Eden*, the Garden of Eden. The first human being, Adam, is placed in a garden of spectacular beauty: "And from the ground the Lord God caused to grow every tree that was pleasing to the sight and good for food, with the tree of life in the middle of the garden, and the tree of knowledge of good and evil" (Genesis 2:9). God intends for Adam to be a farmer, "to till it and tend it." And then God commands Adam: "Of every tree of the garden you are free to eat; but as for the tree of knowledge of good and evil, you must not eat of it; for as soon as you eat of it, you shall die" (Genesis 2:16–17).

The Bible continues with the story of Adam and Eve, the cunning serpent, eating from the forbidden tree, and Adam and Eve's subsequent expulsion from the garden for eating from the one forbidden tree. It is easy, then, to forget that God actually commands eating from *every other* tree, enjoying all the wonderful fruits of the garden. This is the biblical precedent for the Sixth Question you're asked in heaven.

Have you eaten from all the permitted pleasures of the garden?

Rabbi David Lieber points out that the ancient Greek version of the Bible, the Septuagint, translates the word *gan* as *paradeisos,* from the old Persian *pairi-deaza,* meaning "an enclosed park." This is the source of the word *paradise* to describe the garden. The word *eden* means "luxuriance." As Lieber concludes: "Because *eden*

> Did you take full advantage of what you had?
>
> BEN REZNIK

was interpreted to mean 'pleasure,' the word *paradise* took on an exclusively religious connotation as the place of reward for the righteous after death" (*Etz Hayim*, page 14). In other words, *heaven* equals *paradise.* The Garden of Eden was paradise on earth.

A New Food

Rabbi Elazar, commenting on the Sixth Question, is said to have paid particular attention to the direction to enjoy everything permissible by setting aside money so that he could eat every kind of food at least once a year (Jerusalem Talmud, Kiddushin 4:13).

I suppose this is what drives "foodies" to search the world for new and exotic tastes. Tune into the Food Network or travel channels on television for programs that chronicle the culinary adventures of gourmands as they discover the wonders of new foods throughout the world.

This reminds me of one of my favorite Jewish traditions—the celebration of Rosh Hashanah, the New Year, by eating a "new" food. What qualifies the food as "new"? Some say it can be a food that is "new" in the season. For example, in many parts of the world—including my neighborhood!—pomegranates ripen in the fall. A popular choice for the "new" fruit of Rosh Hashanah, pomegranates are said to contain 613 seeds, corresponding to the 613 mitzvot (commandments). Others look for a "new" fruit that is unfamiliar, even exotic. Today, when supermarkets import goods from around the world, many fruits are available year-round. So it becomes a yearly challenge to discover something truly "new." Internet bulletin boards hum with suggestions: lychees, pluots, apriums, apple pears, guava, starfruit, cherimoya. Consult a good greengrocer for suggestions.

> Did you enjoy your life in this world?
> Did you help others to enjoy their life?
>
> DEBBIE STEINBERG

For people celebrating two days of Rosh Hashanah, the actual reason for having a new fruit on the second day is to justify the recitation of the *Shechecheyanu* prayer after the *Kiddush,* thanking God for keeping us alive, sustaining us, and bringing us to the current season. Since Rosh Hashanah is considered one "long day," some rabbis argue that there is no need to recite *Shechecheyanu* on the second night of the holiday. To circumvent that problem, it became a custom to enjoy either a new fruit or to wear a new garment on the second night, either of which can be a cause for reciting the *Shechecheyanu* prayer.

The Day of Abstinence

There is one day in the Jewish year when there is an ascetic sensibility, when there is an attempt to withdraw from all the enjoyments of this world. It is the sacred day of Yom Kippur, the Day of Atonement.

I don't know about you, but I love Yom Kippur. I know it sounds strange, but there is something that is absolutely transformative about this day.

I follow many of the traditional spiritual practices designed to make me focus almost exclusively on the goal of the day—to reckon a personal accounting, a *cheshbon ha-nefesh*, an accounting of the soul. The most obvious of these practices is to deny the body all earthly pleasures.

I fast all day.

I don't wear a watch.

I don't wear leather, a sign of luxury.

I don't bathe, shave, or wear cologne.

I don't engage in intimate relations with my spouse.

She doesn't mind ... since I don't bathe, shave, or wear cologne!

I spend almost the entire day in the synagogue in prayer, study, and reflection.

A neighbor of mine goes one step further. Following tradition, he wears a white garment called a *kittel*. It's not a robe; it's a burial shroud. On Yom Kippur, we rehearse our own deaths. And shrouds have no pockets—all that remains after we die are our souls, our memories, our legacies, our good works.

All this is designed for one purpose: to think about how we will answer the Seven Questions we're asked in heaven, to encourage a serious personal life review—an accounting—that leads to transforming, changing, renewing our lives here on earth.

Yet, after twenty-five hours of self-denial, immediately upon the conclusion of Yom Kippur, we gather with our family and friends and we feast, we celebrate, we enjoy the bounty we are given. We count our blessings, hoping that God will grant us another good year.

A Fish Story

For my family back in Omaha, one of the great events of the year is the annual end-of-Yom-Kippur Break Fast celebration hosted by my cousins Nancy and Don Greenberg. Isn't it funny that in most families, some family members "do Thanksgiving"; some do "Fourth of July"? In our family, Don and Nancy "do Break Fast." More than one hundred people are invited to their beautiful home, most arriving famished from the Yom Kippur fast, eager to enjoy the incredible feast prepared by the Greenbergs.

The feast features many delicacies—Nancy's homemade blintzes, Pam's strudel, Margo's version of "Bubie's cookies" (mandel bread), and Bubie W's famous baby kugels (made in a cupcake tin). But the major food attraction is the smoked-fish delicacies flown in from Barney Greengrass, the Sturgeon King in New York City. For landlocked Jews in Omaha, the Nova lox, whitefish, and pickled herring in cream sauce are quite a treat. Once I introduced Nancy to the pleasures of pickled lox in cream sauce (a marinated filet of salmon smothered in sweet cream and sweet onions—my favorite food *ever!*), she added this *michel* (Yiddish for "delightful food") to the order from Barney's. Suffice it to say that everyone lucky enough to snare an invitation to the Greenbergs' blowout Yom Kippur Break Fast enjoys the permission to, excuse the expression, pig out on fish.

> Good account.
> The goal of Yom
> Kippur.

Once I was visiting New York City on business and arranged to have a meeting at Barney Greengrass on 86th and Amsterdam. After lunch, I went to the front counter to pay the bill (cash only!). Sitting behind the register was a portly elderly man, dressed in a white, open-collar shirt, with his head down, concentrating on the pile of bills and orders spread out on the counter. I later learned that this was the irascible Moe Greengrass, the second-generation owner of Barney's. Hoping to engage him in conversation despite his obvious concern with the business at hand, I said: "Hey, I'm visiting from Los Angeles, but you may know my cousins from Omaha who order fish from you every year for Yom Kippur Break Fast—Don and Nancy Greenberg."

Suddenly, Moe lifted his head, looked me straight in the eye, and, with the deadpan expression of a practiced comedian, said, "Good account."

Good account. The goal of Yom Kippur.

Gifts from God

Did you appreciate God's gifts in this world?

When I ask people whether they have ever had a "spiritual moment" in their lives, they often respond by citing an experience in nature. A gorgeous sunset. A stunning view. A double rainbow at the end of a storm.

Most religious traditions offer a way to recognize these moments with an appropriate prayer thanking God for these gifts. In the Jewish tradition, there are one hundred blessings to be recited each day.

Hmmm. That's a lot of blessings.

Observant Jews attend services three times a day; there are plenty of blessings in the liturgy. Some Jews recite a blessing before eating—the *Motzi*—thanking God for bringing bread from the earth; after the meal, the *Birkat ha-Mazon* has an array of blessings praising God not only for the food eaten but also for things like building Jerusalem and bringing peace.

There are blessings for various natural wonders:

> Smelling fragrant spices, trees, plants, fruits, and oils
>
> Seeing shooting stars, vast deserts, high mountains, and a sunrise
>
> Hearing thunder
>
> Seeing a rainbow
>
> Witnessing trees blossoming
>
> Seeing the ocean
>
> Encountering creatures of striking beauty

And then there are some blessings for unusual suspects:

> Seeing a head of state
>
> Seeing a person distinguished in worldly learning
>
> Seeing a person distinguished in Torah studies
>
> Hearing good news
>
> Hearing bad news
>
> Visiting a place where someone experienced a miraculous rescue

Rabbi Ed Feinstein likes to ask his students to "make up" their own blessings by reflecting on those experiences in life that are wondrous. He will invite a student to tell the story of the experience and then, on the spot, create a blessing to honor the moment.

I remember watching him do this at a Synagogue 2000 conference. A woman stood up and told the moving story of her daughter, Sharon, born with multiple sclerosis, in a wheelchair her entire life, who nevertheless celebrated her bat mitzvah in front of family and friends. As all assembled dissolved in tears, Rabbi Feinstein began to chant:

> "*Barukh ata Adonai, Eloheinu Melekh ha-Olam,*
> [Praised are You, Our God, Sovereign of the Universe,]
> Who enabled Sharon to become a Bat Mitzvah,
> A daughter of Your Commandments,
> Amid her loving family and friends."

And the congregation responded: "*Amen!*"

How do you recognize the blessings in your life?

Speed Bumps

I live in a lovely suburban neighborhood, but quite near a freeway off-ramp. Cars come careening onto Densmore Avenue at a high rate of speed, rushing onto the main thoroughfare of Ventura Boulevard. Our synagogue, Valley Beth Shalom, is four blocks from our home. A day school, a preschool, and an afternoon religious school are on its campus; children walk across Densmore all day long to reach the congregation's parking lot. It is a potentially dangerous situation. Signs are posted: "School Zone," "Danger: Children Crossing." But, mostly, the signs are ignored.

Then, one day, two huge trucks arrived on our street and began to install speed bumps—small hills of asphalt designed to slow down speeding cars. In the middle of each of the four blocks, another speed bump was built. And, lo and behold, cars began to slow down ... and the neighborhood felt safer, slower. Since I travel the street almost every day, I fear what the bumps are doing to my shock absorbers, but I figure it's worth it if the children are out of harm's way.

This is the reason for reciting one hundred blessings every day: to slow us down so we can appreciate what surrounds us.

Why one hundred blessings?

The idea comes from the biblical text:

And now, O Israel, what does the Lord your God, ask of you? Only this: to revere the Lord your God, to walk only in God's paths, to love God, to serve the Lord your God with all your heart and soul, which I enjoin upon you today, for your good.

Deuteronomy 10:12–13

In a commentary on this verse in the Babylonian Talmud, Menachot 43b, the Rabbis point out that if the Hebrew for *what*—*mah*—is read as *mei-ah*—"one hundred"—we can infer that the way to revere God, to be in awe of God, is to recognize all of God's gifts by reciting one hundred blessings each day. Each blessing is a kind of speed bump, slowing us down just enough to appreciate the world around us. The psalmist wrote: *Shiviti Adonai l'negdi tamid*—"I have set God before me constantly" (Psalm 16:8). Each blessing is a rendezvous with God, a way to heighten a personal relationship with heaven as we enjoy the evidence of God's presence on earth.

As Simon and Garfunkel memorably sang: "Slow down. You move too fast."

Mind the speed bumps.

Before I Die

In 1999, an advertising executive and adventure seeker named Dave Freeman and his colleague, Neil Teplica, wrote a book titled *100 Things to Do Before You Die*—and an industry was born. Freeman and Teplica's book was considered a daring gamble; a travel guide with the word *die* in the title. The message of the book was startling: You only have one life to live, the clock is ticking, and there are at least one hundred phenomenal places to visit and amazing events to witness while you can.

In the decade since the book appeared, dozens of similarly themed volumes and articles have been published, promising to guide readers to "can't miss" experiences "before you die":

1,000 Places to See Before You Die

1,000 Things to Do Before You Die

1,000 Recordings to Hear Before You Die

1,000 Unforgettable Senior Moments: Of Which We Could Remember Only 246

1,001 Movies You Must See Before You Die

1,001 Wines You Must Taste Before You Die

1,001 Buildings You Must See Before You Die

20 Hamburgers You Must Eat Before You Die

12 Things to Photograph Before You Die

5 Must-See Events Before You Die

Even Frommer's, the widely respected travel guide publisher, has an entry in this genre, but its title is a bit more subtle—*Frommer's 500 Places to See Before They Disappear*—which may very well have been changed from what I imagine was the original title: *Frommer's 500 Places to See Before* You *Disappear!*

I am sure these guides have their merits; I actually enjoyed skimming through the best known of these books—*1,000 Places to See Before You Die* by Patricia Schultz, mentally checking off those on her list that I have, in fact, seen: Iguaçu Falls in Brazil, Milford Sound in New Zealand, Michelangelo's *David* in Florence, and so on.

> **What do you wish you'd done more of?**
>
> MELANIE STURM

But the real message of the original book was articulated by Neil Teplica when his colleague Dave Freeman unexpectedly and prematurely died at the age of forty-seven. The title of the book meant you should live every day as if it would be your last, and there are not that many people who do, Teplica told the *Los Angeles Times*. "It's a credit to Dave—he didn't have enough days, but he lived them like he should have." The authors wrote in their book: "This life is a short journey. How can you make sure you fill it with the most fun and that you visit all the coolest places on earth before you pack those bags for the very last time?"

Although the authors together visited most of the one hundred sites cited in their book, perhaps the most compelling place in the world for Freeman was not on the list at all. He was born and raised in Los Angeles, and after graduating from the University of Southern California in 1983, he moved to New York City to work in advertising. But on September 11, 2001, while eating breakfast in his sixth-floor apartment, he heard the first plane hit the North Tower of the World Trade Center, located only a few blocks away. Rushing to the roof of his building to see what was happening, Freeman saw the second plane crash into the South Tower. The experience led him to reassess his priorities, and Freeman moved back to Los Angeles in 2002 to be near his family.

Susan's List

The funeral was unlike any I had attended. Our friend Susan Fine had finally succumbed after a five-year battle with cancer at the age of sixty-three. As I approached the small chapel at the cemetery, a large photo montage stood at the front door. Friends gathered around to look at the pictures of family dinners and other occasions. Suddenly, the flat-screen TV used to broadcast the service to overflow crowds outside the chapel came alive with a home video of Susan, her husband, Jerry, and son, Josh, enjoying the many places throughout the world they had visited and the experiences she sought. There they were in China. There they were in Paris. There they were on safari. There they were in Peru. The eulogies emphasized that Susan, a former flight attendant for TWA, loved to travel ... even after the terrible diagnosis of a terminal disease. She was determined to see the world, especially through the eyes of her son, and her list of places to visit was long. At the *shiva*, the videos played on all the televisions in the home, reminding everyone in attendance of Susan's lesson: Do not tarry.

> Stop "killing time" and "wasting time," precious time that you only have one chance to use—to learn, to teach, to create, to hope, to return, to wonder, to lift up.

God's To-Do List

I wrote a book about a list I made. The title is *God's To-Do List: 103 Ways to Be an Angel and Do God's Work on Earth* (Jewish Lights). The message of the book is this: The Jewish answer to the great question "What on earth am I here for?" is that human beings are made in the image of God, to be God's partner in continuing the work of creation and repair. How can you be God's partner? By emulating God's characteristics. Figure out what God does in the Bible, and then do it. And when you do the big and small things that only you, uniquely, can do, you become one of God's angels on earth.

> When you do the big and small things that only you, uniquely, can do, you become one of God's angels on earth.

Made in the image of God means that you have the spark of divinity in you. So if God is creative, you can be creative. If God blesses, you can bless. If God rests, you should rest. If God calls, cares, comforts, and repairs, so can you. If God wrestles, gives, and forgives, so can you. For each of the ten characteristics of God, I suggest ten things that I imagine could be on God's "to-do" list, plus three extra bonus ideas. My suggestions are just that: suggestions, intended to stimulate readers to create their own "God's to-do list." When you do your "to-do's," you can find meaning and purpose in your life.

What's on your God's to-do list?

Your Turn

I have always wondered about the expression: "I'm dying to ..."

"I'm dying to learn how to ski."

"I'm dying to see the Great Wall of China."

"I'm dying to be a grandma."

Shouldn't it be:

"I'm *living* to learn how to ski."

"I'm *living* to see the Great Wall of China."

"I'm *living* to be a grandma."

What are you living to do?

Use the last page of this chapter to make a list of the things you want to do, the places you want to see, the experiences you are *living* to have.

I hope the Sixth Question you're asked in heaven will inspire you to think about the things you want to do to make a difference in the world … or experiences you hope to have during your life.

I hope you will be more aware of the many blessings in your life and, perhaps, you will find a way to acknowledge the privilege of living by offering one hundred blessings each day.

I hope you will stop "killing time" and "wasting time," precious time that you only have one chance to use—to learn, to teach, to create, to hope, to return, to wonder, to lift up.

And, of course, I hope you'll go see God's Alps.

> The whole earth is filled with awe at Your wonders;
> Where morning dawns, where evening fades,
> You call forth songs of joy.
>
> Psalm 65:9

Enjoy God's creation.
All of it that is permitted to you.
Each and every minute.
Today … and every day.

On the next page, I invite you to reflect on your answers to the Sixth Question you're asked in heaven.

What are you living to do? What are the places you want to see? What are the experiences you want to have?

7

Perfecting You

In his classic collection of Hasidic stories, Martin Buber titles this selection "The Query of All Queries":

> Before his death, Rabbi Zusya said: "In the coming world, they will not ask me: 'Why were you not Moses?' They will ask me: 'Why were you not Zusya?'"
>
> *Tales of the Hasidim,* Volume 1, page 251

Indeed, Zusya's question *is* the question of all questions.

It is the Seventh Question you're asked in heaven.

Were you *you?*

Did you live your life trying to be like someone else?

Or …

Were you true to yourself?

Did you use your God-given gifts, talents, and passions to the utmost?

Were you all that you could be?

For heaven will not ask you if you were like Moses … or Einstein … or Mother Teresa … or Madonna … or Kobe Bryant … or Tom Hanks.

No. You'll be asked:

"Were you _____?" (Please write in your name.)

Be All You Can Be

In 1981, the Army recruited the venerable advertising agency N.Y. Ayer and Son to create a new recruiting slogan. The military wanted to emphasize that by enlisting in the volunteer Army you could learn new skills and prepare for a profession, the opportunity to maximize your potential. The memorable tagline was this: "Be all you can be." The catchy jingle went like this: "Be all that you can be! Find your future ... in the Army!" The ads were enormously effective and successful for twenty years. *Advertising Age* magazine ranked "Be all you can be" as the no. 2 jingle of the century, behind McDonald's "You deserve a break today" and ahead of Pepsi's "Pepsi Cola hits the spot."

Not Perfect

Self-improvement is a core value of American individualism. Seemingly from the moment we are born, someone is encouraging us to be all that we can be. Parents want their infants to be "Baby Einsteins," their preteens to be Olympians, and their high schoolers to get into Harvard. Adults attend "one-day universities" and buy self-help courses touted on infomercials. We hire life coaches, gurus, and advisors. Even some clergy build their congregations with the promise of helping people achieve "your best life now."

And we want to look good doing it. So we lift, we tuck, we implant, we whiten, we diet, we exercise. Who doesn't want to look like Angelina Jolie and Brad Pitt? In the movie *The Curious Case of Benjamin Button*, the story of a man born old who ages backward, the character played by Cate Blanchett, upon seeing the young, strappingly handsome Benjamin for the first time, exclaims, "You're perfect!"

I have news for you.

Brad Pitt is not perfect. Neither is Angelina, Cate, or any other movie star.

High-definition television is the worst thing to ever happen to celebrities. The incredibly sharp picture reveals all the wrinkles, spots, and flaws that are evident on every body. Makeup and makeovers may help. Magazines might airbrush imperfections. But the truth is clear.

No body is perfect.
Nobody is perfect.
Not me.
Not you.
Nobody.

Permission Granted

Here is the great insight of Zusya: You are not someone else. You are *you*.

You cannot be Moses. You cannot be Angelina. You cannot be Brad. And once you understand that you are only expected to be you, you have permission to *fail*.

You have permission *not* to be perfect.

You have permission to take risks, to fall down, to come up short—but only in the attempt to be you, not someone else.

Once Zusya realized that he was not expected to be Moses, he could concentrate on being the best Zusya he could be ... not someone bigger or more famous.

A friend told me that the first time he heard the Zusya story, it was like a "whack on the side of the head."

Don't try to be someone you are not.

Be the one you are.

Don't try to be Moses.

Be the best you that you can be.

Perfecting

Perfection is not—cannot—be the goal. Perfecting is.

A well-known Jewish value is popularly known as *tikkun olam*, "repair of the world." The idea comes from the mystical notion that when the world was created, it was perfect. But then it shattered into billions and billions of pieces, leaving it to human beings to work toward repairing the "brokenness." *Tikkun* is translated as "repair."

Usually, the call for *tikkun olam* applies to social justice efforts, community organizing, and communal philanthropy. But there is also the notion of *tikkun atzmi*, perfecting of the self.

"Perfecting" is another translation of the word *tikkun*.

How do you go about perfecting the world?

How do you go about perfecting yourself?

Creating the World, Creating Yourself

As Maria sings in *The Sound of Music*, "Let's start at the very beginning, a very good place to start."

God creates the world in six days and, on the seventh day, God stops creating and rests.

> On the seventh day God finished the work that God had been doing, and God ceased on the seventh day from all the work that God had done. And God blessed the seventh day and declared it holy, because on it God had ceased from all the work that God created to do.
>
> Genesis 2:2–3

This last phrase in Hebrew—*asher bara Elohim la'asot*—is usually translated as "all that God created and made." The upshot is that God ceased from all work that God had done. But the literal translation is "God ceased from all the work that God created to do." Ibn Ezra, a commentator in the Middle Ages, explains that the use of the word *la'asot*—"to do"—indicates that the work of creation was not finished on the seventh day. Rather, God created the basic structures of the world, but God depends on human beings, made in the image of God, to be partners in continuing the ongoing work of creation and repair.

> Perfection is not—cannot—be the goal. Perfecting is.

In his classic book, *The Star of Redemption,* Franz Rosenzweig wrote, "The world is created in the beginning not, it is true, perfect, but destined to have to be perfected."

As we have learned, one path to perfecting yourself is through *teshuvah*—return. If God had made the world and human beings "perfect," well, how boring would that life be? No, the process of return, the act of forgiveness—of others and of oneself—these are the marks of a perfecting person.

Be an Original

My friend Rabbi David Wolpe teaches that the pressure to conform, to be as perfect as the media models we see day in and day out, "the need to fit in often misshapes us." He quotes the poet Edward Young who asked, "Born originals, how comes it to pass that we die copies?" No one needs to reach the standard of someone else. How sad that so often we do not reach the highest level of ourselves. Rabbi Wolpe continues his meditation on the month of Elul, leading up to the High Holy Days:

> The Kotzker Rebbe asked, "If I spend my life pretending to be someone else, who will be me?" This month of Elul is a time to explore our actions, the visible traces of character in this world. If the path we have made is a betrayal of our soul's destiny, we are in need of *tikkun*, of repair. We grow into ourselves so that we return to God as we were made—an end that justifies and completes our beginning.

What are you uniquely able to be, to do, to contribute, to fix? How can you use your unique talents and passions to make a difference, to matter? In perfecting the world, you are perfecting yourself.

Be an original.

Not an imposter.

Don't try to be someone you are not.

One Hundred Pounds

I get a kick out of celebrity look-alikes. A skillful impersonator like Darrell Hammond on *Saturday Night Live* can mimic the mannerisms and voice inflections of famous personalities. There are "tribute bands" like the Fab Four (Beatles), Black Diamond (Neil Diamond), and Purple Reign (Prince). Even I have been mistaken for a Hollywood celebrity—but only after becoming a better me.

I have dealt with weight issues my entire life. A three-time Weight Watcher, I have been on every diet known to humankind. In 1992, I hit my top weight—three hundred pounds. No one wanted to say anything to me as I kept gaining weight. My boss, Dr. David Lieber, may he rest in peace, was the only person who finally said: "Ronnie, I'm worried about your health. We need you around here." It was my wake-up call. And I resolved to set about the task of "perfecting."

The first stop was my doctor's office. He ordered a battery of tests. He was blunt. If I continued on my present course, I was on track to develop high blood pressure and possibly diabetes. Our family history was filled with heart disease; my father had had a major heart attack at age fifty-two. At the time, I was forty-three, with two young children and a terrific wife. Why would I want to take the chance of not being around for them?

There was something else. I was tired. I had begun to give scholar-in-residence weekends, traveling cross-country from Los Angeles. I would come home exhausted on Sunday night. It didn't feel good.

So I made a resolution. It happened to be a "New Year's" resolution. I decided to begin a diet on January 1, 1993. I wanted to be a better, leaner, more energetic me. I had tried to lose weight before ... and I did. But I had always gained back whatever I lost ... and more. This time, I wanted to lose it ... for good.

In six months, I lost eighty pounds. It took another four months to lose the last twenty.

As soon as I tell a crowd that I lost one hundred pounds—and kept it off for fifteen years—nobody wants to hear about my books, my teaching, or my views on anything. All they want to know is "How did you lose one hundred pounds?"

Well, that's the subject of another book. Basically, I ate water-based foods, drank loads of liquids, and ate one small meal in the evening. More important, I changed the way I thought about eating and marshaled the discipline to stick with my new approach.

Do I ever "fall off the wagon"? Sure. I really believe in the two little voices inside me that represent what the Rabbis called the *yeitzer ha-ra*—the inclination to do things that are bad, for you and for others—and the *yeitzer ha-tov*—the inclination to do things that are good, for you and for others.

Most religious and cultural traditions have this notion of the forces for good and evil at work in our spirits. I remember cartoons depicting a character confused by the conflicting advice offered by the "devil" sitting on one shoulder and the "angel" on the other. Or the story told about the Cherokee Indian elder who gives his grandson a warning from the experiences of his life:

> "There are two wolves fighting inside me all the time. The good wolf fights for love and honesty and compassion; the bad wolf fights for hatred and jealousy and greed." As he spoke, his grandson's eyes grew larger and larger. "Grandfather," he asked, "which wolf will win?" The elder paused for a moment and then said, "The one I feed."

I'll tell you one thing. When you lose one hundred pounds, you look totally different. I went from a size 46 waist to a 34. That's twelve inches!

Funny things started to happen. At a scholar-in-residence presentation shortly after I lost the weight, an old friend introduced me, told the audience the story, and then said, "Please join me in welcoming Ron Wolfson, who's half the man he used to be!"

In perfecting the world, you are perfecting yourself.

I didn't feel like "half the man I used to be." Quite the opposite. I felt great, renewed. My teaching was energized. I looked better. In fact, I looked completely different.

Shortly after I lost the weight, Susie and I were invited to a black-tie formal dinner and, of course, I needed a new tuxedo. Sitting at this fancy affair, Susie looked across the table at me and blurted out, "I feel like I'm sleeping with another man!"

One day, I was having lunch at Nate 'n Al's delicatessen in Beverly Hills where a number of celebrities hang out; Larry King has breakfast there almost every morning. Suddenly, a tourist approached my table and asked, "May I have your autograph?" I had no idea why he was asking me. "Oh, Mr. Williams, I just love your movies!" She thought I was the comedian and actor Robin Williams. Personally, I don't see it, but many people do.

I am not Robin Williams. Nor do I want to impersonate him (although he is one of the funniest people on the planet!). I cannot do what he can do, and if I were to try, I would be a pale imitation.

However ...

There is some One I do want to imitate.

I want to imitate God. I want to ignite that spark of divinity in me. I want to animate the "image of God" that I was made to be. I want to activate my *yeitzer ha-tov* as much as possible. I want to work hard at perfecting the world ... and in the process, take another step toward perfecting myself.

> Make the most of yourself, for that is all there is to you.
>
> Ralph Waldo Emerson

How do you go about perfecting yourself?

How do you become the best *you*?

There is no one way, no one magic solution, no one fail-safe method. If there were, the self-help bookshelves at your local bookstore or library would be empty.

It is helpful, though, to think about the major priorities of your life. Our Fifth Question asked you about that. If you are able to get your priorities straight, you may find that there are several places to start.

Here are three:

> Vocations—What is your calling?
>
> Relations—How good are your relationships?
>
> Ministrations—How are you serving others?

Vocations

What are you called to be?

Among the saddest stories I know are those of people who get stuck in jobs they do not enjoy. Plays like *Death of a Salesman* and movies like *Revolutionary Road* illustrate the costs incurred in earlier generations by those toiling away in a vocation that is truly not a calling. In the mid-twentieth century, workers were loyal to their companies and professions, staying with them until retirement.

The educator and philosopher Parker Palmer writes movingly about the toll exacted by staying in the wrong vocation in his book *Let Your Life Speak: Listening for the Voice of Vocation.* After years of disappointment and frustration in the world of academia, Palmer finally looked deep inside himself to discover his true gift. It turned out to be writing. So he left the confines of administration and set out to share his passion for education as an author.

Reflecting on the "church version" of vocation he learned as a child— some external voice telling you what to be—Palmer writes:

> Today I understand vocation quite differently, not as a goal to be
> achieved but as a gift to be received. Discovering vocation does
> not mean scrambling toward some prize just beyond my reach
> but accepting the treasure of true self I already possess. Vocation
> does not come from a voice "out there" calling me to become
> something I am not. It comes from a voice "in here" calling me to
> be the person I was born to be, to fulfill the original selfhood
> given me at birth by God.
>
> *Let Your Life Speak,* page 10

The current generation of young professionals thinks differently about vocation.

I know three young men, all graduates of the best law schools in the land, who have forsaken their training to work in the entertainment industry. Not as attorneys. They want to be screenwriters.

One of these young men, let's call him David, attended an esteemed Ivy League university where he had the opportunity to intern with a major movie studio one summer. His job was to screen screenplays for senior producers, spending hour upon hour reading scripts. He loved it.

> Did you bring joy
> to others?
>
> DEBBIE NEINSTEIN

Then, with the encouragement of relatives, college advisors, and friends, he enrolled in a prestigious law school. Possessing a brilliant mind and plenty of *zitsfleish* (the ability to sit for long periods of time), David worked hard and excelled during the three years of study. Upon graduation, he hoped to land a job in a small law firm doing pro bono work for social justice causes, but the competition for such a position was intense. Instead, he ended up accepting a position as a junior associate in a huge law firm at an incredible six-figure salary, spending hour upon hour reading ... briefs. He was the envy of all his friends, his family was justifiably proud, and he—he was miserable.

> I want to ignite that spark of divinity in me. I want to animate the "image of God" that I was made to be.

David lasted one year. He hated the work, hated the firm, hated the fact that he was twenty-seven years old and not living his dream. So he shocked his friends, his family, and his firm by quitting. Having socked away most of his salary, David decided to listen to his inner calling and set about writing his own screenplay. The last time I spoke with him, he sounded relieved, motivated, and very, very happy.

This is not a new story. The famous painter Paul Gauguin was a stockbroker in Paris and Copenhagen for fourteen years before pursuing his passion for art full time at age thirty-six. Eventually, he moved to the South Sea Islands, where, in 1897, he began work on what became his masterpiece, *Where Do We Come From? What Are We? Where Are We Going?*

Albert Einstein could not find a job in academia upon graduating from ETH Zurich, the Swiss Federal Institute of Technology. So he took a job in the patent office in Berne, Switzerland, as an assistant examiner. He reviewed patent applications for electromagnetic devices. He must not have loved the job, for Einstein was passed over for promotion until he "fully mastered machine technology." In his spare time, he wrote papers outlining his ideas and theories about physics. Eventually, he left patent work to pursue his passion and became the most famous scientist of the twentieth century.

Akiva ben Yosef, known as Rabbi Akiva, is considered one of the most important authorities of the talmudic period. But he did not even begin his own study of Jewish texts until the age of forty! Akiva traveled to the famous academy in Lod, headed by none other than Rabbi Eliezer ben Hyrcanus, the same Rabbi Eliezer who taught, "Repent one day before your death."

Some people have many vocations during their lifetime ... or at least dream of being in a particular line of work.

Like me.

Don't get me wrong. I love what I do—I teach, I write, I speak about subjects I am passionate about. But I occasionally wonder what would have happened if I had chosen a different occupation.

Susie has a term for this.

I love planning and organizing trips; I could easily have been a travel agent. Susie will watch me piece together the puzzle of a journey and she'll say, "Another missed vocation."

I have entrepreneurial DNA; I could easily have been a businessman. Susie will see me promoting this project or that and she'll say, "Another missed vocation."

I enjoy using humorous stories to illustrate my points; I could easily have worked in comedy. When people comment after a lecture, "You should have been a stand-up comedian," Susie will say, "Another missed vocation."

Have you missed your vocation?

Are you working in your dream job?

If not, why not?

Is something ... or someone ... holding you back?

The great Rabbi Hillel said:

> If I am not for me, who will be?
> And if I am for myself alone, what am I?
> And if not now, when?
>
> Pirke Avot 1:14

Relations

Here's the second way you can become a better you: Work on your relationships with others.

Unless you are a monk or a hermit, you spend a good part of your life interacting with other human beings.

This is true, although with all the technological devices of modern living, some people interact more with computers, televisions, and cell phones than they do with real flesh-and-blood people.

How do you engage with another human being? How do you deepen relationships with your spouse, your children, your relatives, your friends, your coworkers?

My teacher on this subject is the twentieth-century philosopher Martin Buber. In his classic work *I and Thou,* Buber presented the idea that all existence was essentially an *encounter* between a human being and an Other. There are two kinds of engagement with the Other: *I-It* and *I-Thou.* In an *I-It* relationship, a person views other people and things as objects to be used. The question is this: How can this person or object serve my interests? In an *I-Thou* relationship, however, two beings encounter each other in their authenticity, not as objects to be used.

The key activity used to create an *I-Thou* relationship is meeting—meeting the Other where she is at, without qualification. This requires seeing the world through the eyes of the Other, understanding how she views the experience of the world. "See it through her eyes," "Stand in his shoes"—these are common sayings that reflect this notion. Buber calls for *dialogue* in an *I-Thou* relationship—a two-way conversation—as opposed to *monologue*—a conversation about yourself.

It was during a Jewish Marriage Enrichment weekend that I first encountered the use of "monologue/dialogue" as a technique to improve the interaction between two lovers, a prime example of an *I-Thou* relationship. Conceived by Rabbi Joseph and Betty Wagner in Los Angeles as a more substantively Jewish experience than Marriage Encounter, the program invited couples to spend a Shabbat weekend together at a beautiful residential camp with the goal of improving communication and deepening relationship. Susie and I were recruited to be the "Jewish content" couple for a number of these weekends, among the most intense and effective educational experiences I have ever known.

After the first session of introductions and welcoming Shabbat on Friday night, three "presenting" couples, trained lay leaders, shared with the group their personal stories of how they met. Then the participants were instructed to go back to their rooms to discuss a topic using a technique called "monologue/dialogue." One person was to speak for fifteen minutes, *without interruption* from the other partner, who was to listen carefully. Then the roles were flipped; the first listener had a chance to speak for fifteen minutes, *without interruption,* while the other partner listened. This turned out to be quite challenging for many of the couples who were used to the give-and-take of daily conversations. After the two monologues, the couples then engaged in a dialogue about what they heard from each other, clarifying each other's points, trying to lovingly understand the other.

As the weekend progressed, the topics of the presentations from the "model" couples progressed from simple issues to much deeper concerns. And as the time allotted to monologue/dialogue increased, the couples built the skill of not just listening, but *hearing* each other. For most, this was difficult interpersonal work. Yet, by the end of the weekend, when the couples were given an hour and a half to write each other a love letter as if it were their last communication, their "last lecture" if you will, the time flew by. After reading each other's letters, the couples engaged in one last dialogue, and often ended up sharing tears of gratitude and affection for the experience of deepening their relationship.

> **Were you good to your parents?**
>
> LARRY NEINSTEIN

What about kids? If you are blessed to interact with children or grandchildren, you know that creating a healthy relationship with them is no simple task.

Here my teacher is Dr. Wendy Mogel, a psychologist from Los Angeles, who wrote a best-selling book, *The Blessing of a Skinned Knee: Using Jewish Teachings to Raise Self-Reliant Children.* She warns of "helicopter" parents, hovering over their very "gifted" children, children who are so coddled and pampered that they are incapable of dealing with frustration, anxiety, or falling down. The resulting dependent children are what college counselors refer to as "teacups" and "krispies," so uncertain of themselves, so fragile that they easily "break" at the slightest hiccup in their perfect lives, especially when they are away from home.

Dr. Mogel counsels parents that the goal of raising "perfect" children as the family "product" leads to "an upside-down, child-centered perspective where we cater to children's whims yet pressure them to achieve at all costs—academically, socially, and athletically." The result: The children find ways to fight back:

> Children who feel they are expected to surpass their parents'
> already high level of achievement or to demonstrate skills that are

beyond their capabilities will suffer. Some children are one-trick ponies: trying to get them to master a broad variety of skills is futile and destructive. Keep at it, and they'll even forget their one trick. Other children begin to feel as if they are working only for their parents' satisfaction, and they openly rebel. Some respond to the pressure by losing their intrinsic enjoyment of mastering skills, and still others use psychosomatic symptoms to get out of the running. By exaggerating their defects, these children hope to avoid failure and to have their progress measured by more individual, realistic standards.

So what are parents to do to establish a nurturing relationship with the child? Dr. Mogel suggests beginning by understanding the Jewish concept that our kids are not solely ours:

Your child is not your masterpiece. According to Jewish thought, your child is not even truly "yours." In Hebrew there is no verb for possession; the expression we translate as "to have," *yesh li*, actually means "It is there for me" or "There is for me." Although nothing belongs to us, God has made everything available on loan and has invited us to borrow it to further the purpose of holiness. This includes our children. They are a precious loan, and each one has a unique path toward serving God. Our job is to help them find out what it is.

She then skillfully outlines several guidelines for raising self-reliant children:

1. Expect differences
2. Learn and accept your child's temperament
3. Stay tuned to gender differences
4. Accept "good enough" for your child
5. Don't pressure yourself to be an extraordinary parent
6. See your child's teacher as an ally
7. Love your children for their own sake

The Jewish tradition recognizes the importance of differences. Think of the "Four Children" in the Passover Haggadah: One is "wise"—a know-it-all—who asks detailed questions about the ritual; one is rebellious, who asks, "What does this mean to you?"; one is "simple, " who asks, "What's it all about?"; and one does not even know how to ask a question.

Let your children be the unique individuals they were created to be.

Every child is gifted … gifted with talents and skills, heart and soul.

Whatever their differences, children crave affection and support from their parents. In our home, we employed two strategies to deepen our relationship with our kids. The first was to bless them every Friday night at the Shabbat table, no matter how badly the week had gone. In my book *Shabbat: The Family Guide to Preparing for and Celebrating the Sabbath* (Jewish Lights), I interviewed a single mom who gave what I think is the most insightful comment about this ritual: "I love blessing my children on Friday night because they have to stand there and take it whether they like it or not." But the import of this act is incalculable. In Judaism, it is not just the rabbis who can bless; you can offer blessings to your children and grandchildren.

> Let your children be the unique individuals they were created to be.

The second strategy comes from Susie's experience as an early childhood educator. Whenever our kids would do something well or something new, we would break out into song:

> We're proud of you,
> So proud of you!
> We're very, very proud of you!
> We hope that *you* are proud of you …
> We're very proud of you, _____ [insert the child's name].

And, don't forget Zadie Louie's self-esteem building technique. Remind them that each one is the best girl or boy in the United States of America!

The term *relatives* is related, of course, to the term *relationship*. Relatives are those who are connected to you by blood or marriage. Siblings, cousins, aunts, uncles, grandparents, nieces, nephews, and the in-laws—

these are the people who make up our families. We see them on holidays, for life-cycle events, and, in some cases, on a regular basis.

There are a lot of jokes made about relatives. At a 2004 Christmas show for troops in Iraq, David Letterman famously quipped: "If I wanted to face insurgents I would've spent Christmas with my relatives." Need I remind you of the hundreds of mother-in-law jokes? They remind us of the tension that often exists in the relationships with others with whom we share a family connection.

Are you close to your relatives? I read of newly discovered relatives who come out of nowhere when someone in the family wins the lottery.

With my family, I won the lottery. My mother and her sisters are as close as relatives can get. They speak on the phone daily; they love and care for each other deeply. Oh, they have their moments; they are not afraid to tell each other their opinion of what the other is doing or not doing. Three of the four siblings are still "alive and kicking," as they like to say, all in their eighties.

When each of the sisters married and began to have children, the extended family grew to nineteen. The gathering place was Bubie Ida and Zadie Louie's home on Miami Street in Omaha, and the main event of the year was the Passover seder. It always seemed a little strange to go to Bubie and Zadie's house dressed up in suits and ties and dresses. Zadie managed to get through the beginning pages of the Haggadah until the Four Questions. After the youngest of the nine grandchildren recited them, Uncle Morton would yell out—every year—the "Fifth Question": "When do we eat?!" That was pretty much the end of the ritual. Zadie would tell Bubie to bring out the feast, coffee was served, and no one ever got back to the table after we had dessert.

The kids would escape to the basement of the house. For us, it was like a huge playground. The favorite game was something we called "War." Teams were chosen and we basically beat each other up. The eldest cousin in the family, Nancy Friedlander, was a few years ahead of most of us, so she did not participate. The only other girl among the nine grandchildren was Laurie Luttbeg. One girl, in the basement with seven boys, playing "War." The evening always ended the same way—Laurie in a car, bleeding, on her way to the emergency room. In fact, today when I see Laurie, I often point out her scars: "See this one on her forehead? Passover 1957.

See this scar on her scalp? Passover 1961. See this scar under her chin? Passover 1963."

Even so, at each of these family gatherings—the holidays, the birthday parties, the performances at school, the ball games—everyone showed up. Our mothers insisted on it. Everybody came to celebrate together, to cheer the others on, to applaud a job well done. And to this day, although we live in different parts of the country and we lead very busy lives, we all show up for the bar and bat mitzvahs and weddings of our cousins and their children and grandchildren. Even at great cost in time and money, we show up. It is quite remarkable, really. But I cannot think of a more important thing to help keep the family relationships strong than to be there for each other.

Are you there for your family?

Do you work on strengthening your relationships with relatives?

What about your relations with friends?

Ina Stein is my wife Susie's friend. A remarkable friend. Ina and Susie met quite by chance at a park in Los Angeles where both had brought their toddler children to play one afternoon. They have been best friends for more than thirty years.

During their weekly coffee date, Ina and Susie regale each other with the stories of their lives. They talk of family, friends, travels, and current events. They celebrate life-cycle events big and small, from weddings to birthdays. They go see movies together featuring Meryl Streep; Ina's husband, Larry, can't stand Meryl Streep.

When Susie was in the hospital, Ina sent flowers to the room and dinner to me. They love to find just the right greeting card for special occasions. They call each other regularly, checking in to make sure all is well.

I asked Susie what it is she loves about her friendship with Ina. "We're on the same page," she replied. "Family is the top priority. We tell each other the continuing stories of our kids, their families, their challenges, their successes. Ina is a great listener. She hears me. She has a great memory for names. And we laugh. A lot. She is so funny. I just love her."

Are you there for your friends?

Do you work on strengthening your relationships with them?

What about your relationships with coworkers?

The main question that I expect in heaven is "Did you live your life for the right purpose?" An excellent answer would be "I helped others to find meaning in life." I believe that we create heaven on earth for other people. By creating a positive legacy through good and noble actions we can create heaven for others. Feeding the hungry; caring for the poor, the sick, and the disadvantaged; creating and promoting peace; educating orphans; empowering women; standing up for the oppressed, and repairing the world are examples of creating heaven on earth for others.

RABBI GERSHOM SIZOMU,
SPIRITUAL LEADER AND ROSH
YESHIVAH, ABAYUDAYA
CONGREGATION, MBALE, UGANDA

In the spring of 1994, I met Dr. Lawrence A. Hoffman in a coffee shop at the dilapidated, recently departed Catskill Mountain resort called the Concord Hotel—may it rest in peace. I had been introduced to him through a mutual friend, Rabbi Rachel Cowan, who knew we shared a similar vision of how synagogues could be transformed into vibrant, engaging sacred communities. We each thought the meeting would be brief, a favor to appease our friend Rachel. But once we sat down together, once we began to tell each other our stories, once we allowed ourselves to dream of a bright future for congregations, the time flew by. Hours later we had agreed to create a new national project in synagogue transformation—Synagogue 2000.

During the past fifteen years, Larry and I have recruited outstanding clergy, educators, artists, and lay leaders; studied congregations across denominations and religious faiths; hired staff; established the first academic research institute exclusively devoted to synagogue studies; traveled the world visiting spiritual communities; written articles and books together and separately; and raised millions of dollars for the effort. Now called Synagogue 3000, our work continues to inform, inspire, and infuse innovation into synagogue life.

We come from different, yet similar worlds: Larry is a rabbi, I am an educator; Larry lives on the East Coast, I live on the West Coast; Larry works primarily in the Reform movement of Judaism, I work primarily in the Conservative movement. We have introduced our best colleagues to each other, creating a unique and valued transdenominational group of visionary leaders who propel our message forward.

Through it all, Larry and I have become the best of friends. Why? Our relationship began with and continues to depend on our willingness to share our life stories with each other. Every phone call, every visit begins with what we call "checking in"—the invitation to listen to our life journeys. We listen without interruption, allowing each other the luxury of *being heard*. We clarify, we empathize, and, when asked, we offer advice to each other. We have laughed together and we have cried together.

Through it all, as remarkable and unbelievable as it may sound, Larry and I have never had a fight or even a serious disagreement. Why? Because we deeply respect each other, we complement each other's strengths, we back up each other's weaknesses. Because we have shared our personal lives, we care for each other. Because we agreed early on that our project would not become the "911 for synagogues," we have had great fun and wonderful experiences. Our work relationship is rooted in our personal relationship. Each of us is a better leader because of the other.

Are you there for your coworkers?

Do you work on strengthening your relationships with colleagues?

The key to a great relationship with others is to stand in their shoes. See the world through their eyes. Figure out their needs. Care for them. And be present when they need you, in the ways that only you can be.

I am always amazed when I pick up Dale Carnegie's famous book, *How to Win Friends and Influence People*. Here are six principles for "making people like you":

1. Become genuinely interested in other people.
2. Smile.
3. Remember that a person's name is to that person the sweetest and most important sound in any language.
4. Be a good listener. Encourage others to talk about themselves.
5. Talk in terms of the other person's interests.
6. Make the other person feel important—and do it sincerely.

All good relationships begin with this recognition: All human beings are made in the image of God. Greet other people. Remember their names.

Ask about their story. Stand in their shoes. Care for them. Be a good friend in your own unique way.

Ministrations

If *vocations* is about finding your true calling and *relations* is about improving your relationships, *ministrations* is about serving or aiding others.

How are you serving your fellow human beings?

There are many ways to "repair the world." The prophetic call for social justice rings true in the hearts of most human beings. The religious imperative to minister to others is a bedrock value in most faith traditions. To be fully human is to recognize the plight of those less fortunate than you—and to do something about it.

That is why part of the Seventh Question you are asked in heaven concerns what you fixed on earth.

What did you fix?

Did you use your unique God-given gifts, skills, passions, and resources to be a "repair person"?

Fortunately, the Jewish tradition offers a "toolbox," holding a variety of instruments to fix the brokenness in the world.

I learned one of the first of these tools when I was a young boy attending Beth El Synagogue Hebrew School. Every year, our teachers handed us a sheet of cardboard with the words *Plant a Tree in Israel* written across the top. It was a fund-raising tool from the Jewish National Fund. The cardboard had perforated slots to hold coins—nickels, dimes, and quarters—that added up to $3. Every day we came to Hebrew school, we were told to bring some coins to fill in the slots. When the card was filled, we were able to buy a tree to be planted in Israel. And we could choose to whom we wished to dedicate the tree: a parent, a grandparent, or a friend. The dedication was duly typed onto a formal certificate, which we then presented to the person we honored. Oh, we had those little "blue boxes" to collect money as well. But the tree campaign was much more fun.

When I became a teenage activist in United Synagogue Youth, our synagogue youth group, I discovered new ways to repair the world. We served food to the homeless on Christmas Day, visited the elderly folks at the

Home for the Aging, and spent an afternoon picking up trash near the sides of the roads. I remember how thrilled and proud I felt when a photo of the March on Selma was published in newspapers all over the world and there, standing arm and arm in the front row near Dr. Martin Luther King Jr., was my rabbinic hero, Abraham Joshua Heschel. When asked what it was like to participate in the march, Heschel replied, "I felt like my legs were praying."

> We are called upon to be an image of God. You see, God is absent, invisible, and the task of a human being is to represent the Divine.

Once I was in college in the late sixties, the tumult of the Vietnam War weighed heavily on me. I joined hundreds of students in protesting the war; I even joined a sit-in at the administration building at Washington University. As a student leader of the Hillel Foundation, I had the opportunity to meet Rabbi Heschel. He was scheduled to lecture at Graham Chapel in the Distinguished Speaker Series and, through the student grapevine, I learned that if you invited Heschel to participate in a worship service, a minyan, he would attend. So I wrote him a letter and, sure enough, Heschel wrote back that he would come. After the prayers concluded, he sat with us for a few minutes of conversation. Always the teacher, he encouraged us to remember our responsibility to work for social justice. As he told ABC News shortly before his untimely death at the age of sixty-five:

> We are called upon to be an image of God. You see, God is
> absent, invisible, and the task of a human being is to represent
> the Divine, to be a reminder of the presence of God.

In her insightful book, *There Shall Be No Needy: Pursuing Social Justice through Jewish Law and Tradition* (Jewish Lights), Rabbi Jill Jacobs surveys the entire gamut of texts illuminating the Jewish values underlying the call for social justice. She zeroes in on seven of the major concerns in society today: relieving poverty; collecting and allocating charity dollars; worker's rights; homelessness; health care; environmental sustainability; and crime, punishment, and rehabilitation. Rabbi Jacobs offers three core principles that animate the Jewish position: (1) the dignity of human life because every person is "made in the image of God," (2) the consequences of the disparity in power among economic and social classes, and (3) the individual's responsibility to the community and the concomitant responsibility of the community to take care of individuals.

Rabbi Jacobs points out that the selection of Prophets read on the most sacred day of the Jewish year, Yom Kippur, is a warning that fasting, spiritual practice, even the observance of commandments cannot supersede the imperative to work for social justice:

> Why, when we fasted, did You not see? When we starved our bodies, did You pay no heed? Because on your fast day you see to your business and oppress all your laborers! Because you fast in strife and contention, and you strike with a wicked fist! Your fasting today is not such as to make your voice heard on high. Is such the fast I desire, a day for men to starve their bodies? Is it bowing the head like a bulrush and lying in sackcloth and ashes? Do you call that a fast, a day when Adonai is favorable? No, this is the fast I desire: to unlock the fetters of wickedness, and untie the cords of the yoke to let the oppressed go free; to break off every yoke. It is to share your bread with the hungry, and to take the wretched poor into your home; when you see the naked, to clothe him, and not to ignore your own kin.
>
> Isaiah 58:3–7

What are you doing to make a difference in the lives of others?

I offer an example. One fall semester, I met my class of incoming graduate students in the Fingerhut School of Education at the American Jewish University. There were twelve young women … or, at least … I thought there were twelve. As we circled the room for introductions, one of the students announced that his name was "Noam." I thought I heard "Noa," but no, it was "Noam." She was a he … a he with striking black hair that cascaded over his shoulders, nearly reaching his waist. Taken aback, I certainly did not want to challenge his choice of hairstyle … and the semester proceeded. Three weeks before the class concluded, Noam e-mailed me an invitation to an *upshirin*. In some traditional Jewish circles, a boy's hair is not cut until he reaches three years old. Then, in a wonderful communal celebration, the first haircut is performed in front of family and friends. Noam was not three; he was twenty-three. Nevertheless, the invitation was for *his upshirin!* Noam Raucher had been growing his hair for months after learning about "Locks of Love," a not-for-profit organization that collects donated hair to make into wigs for children with conditions such as alopecia areata who will never grow their natural hair again and some cancer survivors. It was a simple, but unique ministration.

What are your ministrations?

How to Be the Best

In his book, *Outliers,* Malcolm Gladwell considers the question of how the "best" at something comes to be that way. What makes for success? While acknowledging that a variety of factors—birth, culture, circumstance, and historical legacy—account for success, two things struck me about his argument. Echoing the old question I remember from my childhood—"How do you get to Carnegie Hall?"—Gladwell's answer is the same: "Three ways: Practice, practice, practice." He claims that "the best" have spent a minimum of ten thousand hours learning a skill, achieving mastery over their subjects, over their bodies, over their God-given talents.

> How many people did you help? Did you help in ways that reflect your uniqueness?
>
> JANICE KAMINER-REZNIK

But, there's more to being the best than that. You've got to have what my mother calls *mazel*—"luck." Be in the right place at the right time. Know the right people.

Yet, Gladwell insists, if you are not ready at the "right time," if you are not prepared when you meet the "right people," you may not "be your best" when you most need to be.

I thought of this when, on a frigid afternoon in 2009 in New York City, US Airways Flight 1549, climbing out of LaGuardia airport, hit a flock of birds, knocking out both engines. The pilot, Chesley "Sully" Sullenberger, a forty-year veteran with many more than ten thousand hours of flying experience and a passion for airline safety issues, took the controls of the crippled plane with 155 human beings aboard and calmly, skillfully landed it in the icy Hudson River. Everyone survived, hailing Captain Sullenberger as the hero. The media called it the "Miracle on the Hudson," and indeed it was. But this time, God had a copilot. In fact, five copilots: All five people on the crew that day were veterans, well trained and well prepared to be their best at the very moment when they most needed to be.

Chaim's Trumpet

My beloved mentor, Rabbi Bernard Lipnick, told me an incredible story about perfecting. Here it is in the words of a grateful grandfather:

The news was devastating. Corinne and Jesse had noticed some irregular-ities in my grandson, Chaim, their fourteen-month-old child. He seemed to have a runny nose all the time and, generally, to be somewhat sickly. When the test results did come back, the diagnosis was far worse than any-thing they could have imagined. Chaim was afflicted with cystic fibrosis.

Cystic fibrosis is a terrible genetic disease that mainly affects the lungs, causing difficulty in breathing and maintaining normal weight and growth. When Chaim was diagnosed, Corinne and Jesse were told that the average life expectancy of such children was only twenty-eight years.

Jesse, Chaim's father, is a physician and Corinne is a therapist. Both par-ents, therefore, were keenly aware of the medical realities and the kind of response they would need to have in order to raise their son as healthfully and normally as possible. They both immersed themselves in a careful analysis of the disease and what it was that they had to do in order to help Chaim face the formidable challenges that lay before him.

At that time, one of the main treatments for cystic fibrosis was per-cussing—a series of poundings to the chest and back in an attempt to loosen the thickened mucus in the child's lungs. Doctors advised that the percussing should be done three or four times every day, in five different positions, with three minutes devoted to each position for a total of four fifteen-minute sessions of, literally, beating the child's upper torso. Needless to say, Chaim was far from enamored of this therapy. When he realized that it was time for his percussing to begin, Chaim would do everything in his power to avoid it. He would run away and hide. He shed many, many tears before he could be cajoled into subjecting himself to this painful routine.

Corinne and Jesse would do everything they could to soften these per-cussing sessions, but the plain fact is that when a child is beaten on a reg-ular basis, even though it is out of love for his own good, he begins to show signs of what might be called battered or abused child syndrome.

When Chaim started school, he gave every indication of being very bright, yet his performance in school was somewhat spotty. Were the years of physical beating that he had endured, and was still enduring, somehow related to this poor performance? Constantly on the lookout for new methods of dealing with Chaim's lung problem, Corinne came up with a thought. Perhaps learning to play a wind instrument would have a beneficial effect on Chaim's lungs and preclude the need for the constant percussing. She acquired a used trumpet and urged Chaim to try it out. He did and, wouldn't you know it? He seemed to "take" to the instrument. Pretty soon, not only did he demonstrate pleasure in playing the trumpet, but he showed some genuine talent and real aptitude.

Upon entering middle school, Chaim decided that he would try out for its band. His parents helped by providing him with professional trumpet lessons. The more he played the trumpet, the more he enjoyed himself. Amazingly, the need for stimulating his lungs in an artificial manner grad-ually decreased … and the dreaded percussing stopped.

After his parents moved mountains to have him admitted to Buchholz High School, Chaim tried out for its award-winning marching band. He was accepted, but on one condition. To remain a member of the band, he had to make good grades. Suddenly, the motivation of remaining in the band was sufficient to inspire Chaim to do excellent work in all his classes. No more battered child excuses for poor performance.

As of now, Chaim is a sophomore at Buchholz. In addition to the marching band, he is a trumpeter in the wind symphony, the highest-level orchestra in the school. In April 2009, Chaim Lipnick was going to be playing trumpet during a concert competition in New York City's famed Carnegie Hall!

More important, Chaim has fared extremely well with his cystic fibro-sis. He has grown into a handsome five-foot-eleven young man and his lung function is normal in every way. And all because of the kind of par-ents he is blessed with—and Chaim's trumpet, which has become such an integral part of his life!

A More Perfect Self

I write these words on the eve of January 20, 2009, the day the people of the United States of America inaugurated their forty-fourth president, Barack Obama, a day I never believed I would witness in this lifetime. As a teenager, I lived through and worked for the struggle for civil rights. I mourned the assassinations of President John F. Kennedy, Dr. Martin Luther King Jr., and Robert F. Kennedy. I cried when three civil rights workers—Andrew Goodman, twenty; Michael Schwerner, twenty-four; and James Chaney, twenty-one—two white Jews from New York and a black resident of Mississippi—were murdered by the Ku Klux Klan in 1964.

For an African-American to become the president of the United States is, indeed, a historic milestone on the path to forming "a more perfect Union," the clarion call of the Preamble of the Constitution. Throughout his campaign for the presidency, Barack Obama inspired the American people to unite in common cause to "perfect" the Union—by committing themselves to serve others, to see every citizen as free and equal, to agree to disagree with civility and respect, to discover our shared values and strengths to meet the daunting challenges facing the country at the dawn of the new year. His first official act as president was to declare the day of his inauguration as a National Day of Renewal and Reconciliation, calling on "all our citizens to serve one another and the common purpose of remaking this nation for our new century," to continue the work of perfecting the Union.

What are you perfecting?

In 1987, an educator named Michael Josephson established the Josephson Institute, named after his parents—to "improve the ethical quality of society by changing personal and organizational decision making and behavior." The program that put the institute on the map, "Character Counts," has been adopted by school districts, businesses, sports teams, and civic organizations across the country.

In the mid-nineteenth century, Israel Salanter, a rabbi in Lithuania, began a movement to improve the character of his disciples. It is called *Mussar,* literally "instruction." The *Mussar* literature seeks to instill greater piety and ethical conduct in personal behavior, leading to a more reflective, meaningful life.

Here are some of the traits that Alan Morinis in his book, *Everyday Holiness: The Jewish Spiritual Path of Mussar,* suggests for a life review:

1. *Humility*—Do you act humbly?
2. *Patience*—Are you able to summon patience in moments of frustration?
3. *Gratitude*—Are you grateful for all that is given you?
4. *Compassion*—Do you care for others?
5. *Order*—Is your life organized?
6. *Equanimity*—Can you cultivate a sense of contentment even when things are not perfect?
7. *Honor*—Do you elevate those around you?
8. *Simplicity*—Do you keep it simple?
9. *Enthusiasm*—Do you bring energy to all your endeavors?
10. *Silence*—Do you have an island of quiet in your life?
11. *Generosity*—Are you giving of yourself and your resources?
12. *Truth*—Have you been honest with yourself and others in both word and deed?
13. *Moderation*—Is there balance in your life?
14. *Loving-kindness*—Do you perform selfless acts?
15. *Responsibility*—Have your actions added to justice in the world?
16. *Trust*—Can people count on you?
17. *Faith*—Do you believe?
18. *Yirah*—Do you see the awesomeness of God's universe?

Use these questions as you go about the task of perfecting yourself and the world around you.

Here is one more way to work on perfecting yourself.

You can admit that, sometimes, you goof up.

Sometimes, you don't do the right thing.

Sometimes, you do the wrong thing.

During the Yom Kippur holiday, the liturgy includes the *Al Chet*, a recitation of a long list of more than fifty "sins"—eating too much, gossiping, dishonesty, and the like. The traditional ritual calls for a symbolic beating of the chest with a clenched fist as each transgression is recalled. Punctuating the list is the famous formula for seeking repentance: *"V'al kulam eloha s'lichot, s'lach lanu, m'chal lanu, kahper lanu*—For all these [sins], O God of forgiveness, forgive us, pardon us, grant us atonement."

A similar scenario unfolds during the *Ashamnu*, the communal confessional of sins. The words are recited in the plural—"We have offended, we

have strayed, we have robbed, we have been mean, violent, and false ..."
Once again, the beating of the chest emphasizes the urgency of the
moment.

In the Jewish tradition, this process is not just a once-a-year event; it is
a *daily* event. In the traditional morning *Amidah,* the liturgy reads:
"Forgive us, our Ancestor, for we have sinned. Pardon us, our Sovereign,
for we have transgressed. You forgive, You pardon. Praised are You, gracious and forgiving God." As the words *s'lach lanu* and *m'chal lanu* are
recited, once again, traditional Jews beat their chests.

There is an underlying promise in these ritual confessions. It is the
promise of forgiveness. Forgiveness from God. Forgiveness from those
who have been wronged.

And forgiveness can be a critical component in the process of perfecting yourself.

What is the path that leads to forgiveness?

Begin by reviewing all the aspects of your life. Ask yourself whether you
are the best *you* you can be.

Admit that no one is perfect. Not even you.

Make a list of your goof-ups, your own litany of *Al Chets.*

Be honest with God. Be honest with others. Be honest with yourself.

If any of the goof-ups involve other human beings, ask for forgiveness—from them, not just from God. Make restitution. Make amends.
Make up. Make it right.

Work on perfecting your relationships.

Every day.

It is one more way toward perfecting yourself.

Go to Yourself

One of my favorite portions of the Torah is *Lech Lecha.* It begins:

> The Lord said to Abram: "Go forth from your native land and
> from your father's house to the land that I will show you. I will
> make of you a great nation, and I will bless you. I will make your
> name great, and you shall be a blessing.
>
> Genesis 12:1–2

The words *Lech Lecha* are usually translated as "Go forth." But the literal translation is "go to yourself." A midrash suggests that the call to Abraham was not simply to leave everything he knew and follow God to "a land that I will show you." Rather, this is a call to "Go forth and discover your authentic self, to learn who you are meant to be" (*mei ha-shi-loach*).

Do you know yourself?

Are you aware of your journey?

Believe it or not, some people go through life completely unreflective, blissfully unaware of their impact in the world.

Until they get to heaven.

And then they are asked:

"Were you the best you you could be?"

Did you reach your potential as a human being?

Did you know yourself—your vocations, your relations, your ministrations?

The Seventh Question you are asked in heaven invites you to reflect on your *Lech Lecha* journey.

Find your authentic self.

You have permission to take the risk to learn who you are meant to be.

Remember:

When you get to heaven, you will not be asked:

"Were you like Moses?"

You will not be asked:

"Were you like Zusya?"

When you get to heaven, you will be asked:

"Were you _____?" (Please fill in your name.)

On the next page, I invite you to reflect on your answers to the Seventh Question you're asked in heaven.

THE QUESTIONS ARE THE ANSWERS

D o you want to know how to live a life well lived?
Embedded within the Seven Questions you're asked in heaven are the answers.

Each of us will answer the questions differently.

The important thing is to ask them of yourself now.

Heaven can wait.

The poet Rainer Maria Rilke wrote:

I want you, as much as you can ... to be patient toward all that is unsolved in your heart and to try to love the questions themselves like locked rooms and like books that are written in a very foreign tongue. Do not seek the answers that cannot be given you because you would not be able to live them. And the point is to live everything. Live the questions now. Perhaps you will then gradually, without noticing it, live along some distant day into the answer.

Letters to a Young Poet, Letter Four (July 16, 1903)

Escaping Death

On September 1, 1939, my father-in-law, Abram Kukawka, was a young man living in a small village called Slawiticze, Poland, with his parents, Michel and Sure; three married sisters, Mariyam, Jospe, Frime; and a younger brother, Gedalya (George). That day, the Nazis invaded Poland from the west; Slawiticze was on the eastern border of Poland, near the Buk River. Realizing the impending danger, Abe's mother told the two boys to escape into Russia. Reluctantly, they crossed the river—and never saw their parents, sisters, or their families again. All were murdered by the Nazis.

Abe has been escaping death ever since.

Miraculously, Abe survived the war, working as a valet to a sympathetic colonel in the Russian army. In 1945, he made his way to Berlin, reuniting with his brother and meeting Hildegarde Lieball, a young Jewish woman who had been hidden by a Christian family in a farming community in the German countryside. They married, had a baby named Sure (Susie), and immigrated to the United States, where they were placed in the Jewish community of Omaha, Nebraska. With no English and no money, Abe found work in a factory making hydraulic pumps, a job he kept for twenty-five years.

> Did you make a
> difference?
>
> SUSIE WOLFSON

When Abe retired, Susie and I gave him a gift—a membership in the local Jewish Community Center health club. He had never had time to work out; he worked every minute of overtime he could get. But now he could spend some time on himself. Abe was sixty-five years old when he first walked into the "J." He threw himself into exercise classes, and began to run mini-marathons, lift weights, and swim laps.

Today, Abe is approaching his one hundredth birthday, which, God willing, we will celebrate on April 10, 2010. He is in terrific shape for a man of his age. Twice he escaped death from heart disease, enduring not one, but two open-heart surgeries to bypass diseased arteries and replace two worn heart valves. Abe was ninety-five when he had the second valve replacement at the world-famous Mayo Clinic. In the weeks leading up to the surgery, Abe bought himself a brand new car—and insisted on a ten-year warranty! He told the Mayo heart surgeon he wanted the same deal on his new heart valve.

In Omaha, Abe has become something of a legend. He lives in the Rose Blumkin Jewish Home, which is contiguous to the JCC. Twice a day, he walks the equivalent of two blocks through the hallways to his beloved health club where he works out, takes a *shvitz*—steambath—and showers. He occupies locker number 1, and the lawyers, doctors, and businessmen who frequent the place adore him.

When people ask Abe his secret for living so long, he tells the following story, in his inimitable Yiddish accent:

> Vell, do you know who the *malach ha-maves* is? The *malach ha-maves* is the Angel of Death. Now, he's a kinda lazy guy ... but every day, the *malach ha-maves* has a quota ... he's gotta bring in a certain number of people. But, he doesn't like to work too hard. So he looks for a lazy one ... someone sitting on the couch, eating potato chips, watching television. Easy catch! But if he sees that you're moving, runnin' ... well, he figures, "I'm not runnin' after him. I'll catch him some other time." So ... keep moving!

Immortality

You don't have to die.

Oh, your body will die.

But not your soul.

Not your legacy.

Not your memory.

Not your influence.

How you live your life now will determine your life after death.

Will you be remembered? Will your good works continue? Will your children and grandchildren honor your name?

I believe this for one reason. I believe we are born with the spark of divinity within each of us, each of us made in the image of God.

The Seven Questions you're asked in heaven are God's way of reminding you that the answers lie within.

The midrash teaches:

When God set out to create Adam, the first human being, God told the angels: "I will make human beings in My image." The angels were outraged. How can something so precious, so powerful be entrusted to this creature? If humans have the Divine Image, they will think like God thinks, feel what God feels, create as God creates, and, most shocking of all, they will grasp eternity and live forever, just as God lives forever. We cannot let this happen!

So the angels conspired to steal and hide the Divine Image somewhere where human beings would never find it. The question was: Where?

"Let us put it at the top of the highest mountain," one angel suggested. The others replied: "No, they will learn to climb the highest mountain and find it." "Let us put it at the bottom of the sea," another offered. "No," the others replied, "they will plumb those depths one day and find it."

One by one, the angels made suggestions, but each one was rejected. Finally, the cleverest of the angels had an idea: "Let us place the Divine Image within the human heart, within the soul. They'll never find it there."

And so the angels hid the precious Divine Image within the heart of human beings, where it lies hidden to this day.

As my teacher, Rabbi Harold Schulweis, concludes:

> Immortality is not found in heaven. It is not on the top of the mountains, or the bottom of the sea. It is here in our hearts, in the way we live.... Look within you and find the immortality that God has planted there.

The Seven Questions

Let's take one last look at the Seven Questions you're asked in heaven.

The First Question: Were you honest?

The Second Question: Did you leave a legacy?

The Third Question: Did you set a time to study?

The Fourth Question: Did you have hope in your heart?

The Fifth Question: Did you get your priorities straight?

The Sixth Question: Did you enjoy this world?

The Seventh Question: Were you the best *you* you could be?

Now you have a choice.

You can look at your life so far and answer the questions.

Or you can look forward and ask yourself: "How can I get to 'yes'?"

How can I be more honest—in my business, in my relationships, with myself?

How can I leave a legacy—make a difference, become an ancestor?

How can I find time to study—to learn from everyone and every experience?

How can I have hope—in times of trouble, to believe that better days are ahead?

How can I prioritize—my time, my efforts, my goals?

How can I enjoy—everything permitted to me, the beauty and the blessings of God's creation?

How can I be me—fulfilling my unique potential, in my job, with family and friends, by serving others?

One Hour

A remarkable passage in Pirke Avot reminds us that the Seven Questions are not about heaven at all. They are designed to focus you not on the *after*life, but on *this* life.

What will happen in the next life?

Who knows?

The only thing we can do is make this life matter.

Better is one hour of *teshuvah* and good works in this world than
the whole life of the world to come.

Pirke Avot 4:22

Here … in this world … you can make a difference.
  Believe in life before death.
  Ask yourself the Seven Questions.
  Work toward answering them affirmatively—
  today, and …
  when you get to heaven.

ꙮ NOTE TO READERS

The Seven Questions You're Asked in Heaven presents Jewish wisdom for people of all faiths. Although the Seven Questions emerge from the imaginations of Rabbis throughout the ages, every faith tradition has envisioned what might be asked of one who reaches heaven. These questions are designed to stimulate a reviewing—and a renewing—of your life on earth.

This "life review" can be done at any moment, but there are "prime times" in the calendar that invite this work. For Jews, the period of the High Holy Days—the Ten Days of Return—is a wonderful opportunity for personal reflection and spiritual renewal. You may be invited by your congregation to participate in a "community read" between Rosh Hashanah and Yom Kippur, or perhaps, in the month of Elul, the spiritual lead-up to the New Year. Your rabbi may choose to speak about the themes in the book during the holidays. You may be asked to complete the worksheets at the end of each chapter, enabling you to put in writing your personal *cheshbon ha-nefesh*—"spiritual accounting of the soul." For Christians, the end-of-year holidays of Christmas and New Year's and the Easter celebrations are excellent times to review and renew your life's journey. Truly, any time is a good time to engage in personal reflection.

I hope you will find *The Seven Questions You're Asked in Heaven* provocative and challenging!

✑ SUGGESTIONS FOR FURTHER READING AND SOURCES CITED

Beamer, Lisa. *Let's Roll! Ordinary People, Extraordinary Courage*. Carol Stream, Ill.: Tyndale, 2002.

Buber, Martin. *I and Thou*. New York: Touchstone, 1970.

———. *Tales of the Hasidim*. New York: Schocken Books, 1991.

Carnegie, Dale. *How to Win Friends and Influence People*. New York: Pocket Books, 1936.

Comins, Mike. *A Wild Faith: Jewish Ways into Wilderness, Wilderness Ways into Judaism*. Woodstock, Vt.: Jewish Lights Publishing, 2007.

Dorff, Elliot N. *The Way Into Tikkun Olam (Repairing the World)*. Woodstock, Vt.: Jewish Lights Publishing, 2007.

Frank, Anne. *The Diary of Anne Frank*. New York: Doubleday, 1969.

Frankl, Viktor. *Man's Search for Meaning*. Boston: Beacon Press, 1959.

Freeman, Dave, and Neil Teplica. *100 Things to Do Before You Die: Travel Events You Just Can't Miss*. New York: Cooper Square Press, 1999.

Gladwell, Malcolm. *Outliers: The Story of Success*. New York: Little, Brown and Company, 2008.

Gruman, Jessie. *AfterShock: What to Do When the Doctor Gives You—Or Someone You Love—a Devastating Diagnosis*. New York: Walker and Company, 2007.

Heschel, Abraham Joshua. *Man Is Not Alone*. New York: Farrar, Straus and Giroux, 1951.

Jacobs, Jill. *There Shall Be No Needy: Pursuing Social Justice through Jewish Law and Tradition*. Woodstock, Vt.: Jewish Lights Publishing, 2009.

Josephson, Michael. *The Power of Character*. San Francisco: Jossey-Bass, 1998.

Lieber, David L. *Etz Hayim: Torah and Commentary*. Philadelphia: Jewish Publication Society, 2001.

Mogel, Wendy. *The Blessing of a Skinned Knee*. New York: Scribner, 2001.

Morinis, Alan. *Everyday Holiness: The Jewish Spiritual Path of Mussar*. Boston: Trumpeter, 2007.

Obama, Barack. *The Audacity of Hope*. New York: Crown Publishing Group, 2006.

Palmer, Parker. *Let Your Life Speak: Listening for the Voice of Vocation*. San Francisco: Jossey-Bass, 2000.

Pausch, Randy. *The Last Lecture*. New York: Hyperion, 2008.

Rilke, Rainer Maria. *Letters to a Young Poet* (translated by Stephen Mitchell). New York: Random House, 1984.

Rosenzweig, Franz. *The Star of Redemption*. Madison: University of Wisconsin Press, 2005.

Rosten, Leo. *The Joys of Yiddish*. New York: McGraw Hill, 1968.

Schultz, Patricia. *1,000 Places to See Before You Die: A Traveler's Life List*. New York: Workman, 2003.

Shanley, John Patrick. *Doubt* (movie tie-in edition). New York: Theater Communications Group, 2008.

Telushkin, Joseph. *Jewish Wisdom*. New York: William Morrow, 1994.

Wolfson, Ron. *God's To-Do List: 103 Ways to Be an Angel and Do God's Work on Earth*. Woodstock, Vt.: Jewish Lights Publishing, 2006.

———. *Shabbat: The Family Guide to Preparing for and Celebrating the Sabbath,* 2nd ed. Woodstock, Vt.: Jewish Lights Publishing, 2002.

———. *The Spirituality of Welcoming: How to Transform Your Congregation into a Sacred Community*. Woodstock, Vt.: Jewish Lights Publishing, 2006.

Wolpe, David. *Why Faith Matters*. New York: Harper One, 2008.

ACKNOWLEDGMENTS

My thanks to colleagues and friends who contributed ideas and stories for this project: Rabbis Harold Schulweis, Elliot Dorff, Elie Spitz, Bernard Lipnick, Jill Jacobs, Jack Riemer, Ed Feinstein, Gershom Sizomu, and David Wolpe. The contributions from Craig Taubman, Judy Bin-Nun, Richard Joel, Judy and Lou Miller, Ted Plavin, Neshama Carlebach, Debbie Steinberg, Michael Brooks, Leia and Dwight Smith, Melanie Sturm, Hope Levy, Barb Burg, and our *chavurah*—Debbie and Larry Neinstein, Janice and Ben Reznik, Tobi and Nachum Inlender, Nan and Richard Zaitlen, and Beverly Weise—illuminate the text. During a delightful visit with the staff of Jewish Lights Publishing in Woodstock, Vermont, Antoinette and Stuart M. Matlins encouraged me to write the book. Once again, the extraordinary staff at Jewish Lights, especially Emily Wichland, took my words and shaped an appealing volume.

I am blessed with a loving family who continue to support all that I do: Bernice and Alan Wolfson, Abe Kukawka, Bob and Sibby Wolfson, Doug and Sara Wolfson, Aunt Rose Rosen, Aunt Ruth Luttbeg, Nancy and Don Greenberg, Pam and Bruce Friedlander, Margo Rosen, Joan Rosen, Linda and Steve Luttbeg, and Laurie and Mark Spiegler. Susie Kukawka Wolfson is my life partner and my source of inspiration; words are inadequate to express my love for you.

Beginning in the Bible, there is a tradition of parents writing a letter to their children to share life lessons learned. Jacob calls his sons to his bedside to project their futures. Moses offers a stirring farewell address to the people Israel. Throughout Jewish literature, there are numerous examples of these ethical wills. Perhaps even more meaningful than possessions, leaving behind a legacy of wisdom to one's descendants is a profoundly personal act. I have dedicated this book to my descendants, who include, so far, Michael Louis Wolfson and the newlyweds, Havi Michele Wolfson and David Hall. (For readers of *God's To-Do List*, Dave *did* ask for our blessing and we lovingly gave it!) May you and all my future descendants be blessed with lives that strive to answer the Seven Questions in purposeful and meaningful ways.

Ron Wolfson

Pastoral Care Resources
LifeLights/™אורות החיים

LifeLights/™אורות החיים are inspirational, informational booklets about challenges to our emotional and spiritual lives and how to deal with them. Offering help for wholeness and healing, each *LifeLight* is written from a uniquely Jewish spiritual perspective by a wise and caring soul—someone who knows the inner territory of grief, doubt, confusion and longing.

In addition to providing wise words to light a difficult path, each *LifeLight* booklet provides suggestions for additional resources for reading. Many list organizations, Jewish and secular, that can provide help, along with information on how to contact them.

Categories/Sample Topics:

Health & Healing
Caring for Yourself/When Someone Is Ill
Facing Cancer as a Family
Recognizing a Loved One's Addiction, and Providing Help

Loss / Grief / Death & Dying
Coping with the Death of a Spouse
From Death through Shiva: A Guide to Jewish Grieving Practices
Taking the Time You Need to Mourn Your Loss
Talking to Children about Death

Judaism / Living a Jewish Life
Bar and Bat Mitzvah's Meaning: Preparing Spiritually with Your Child
Yearning for God

Family Issues
Grandparenting Interfaith Grandchildren
Talking to Your Children about God

Spiritual Care / Personal Growth
Easing the Burden of Stress
Finding a Way to Forgive
Praying in Hard Times

Now available in hundreds of congregations, health-care facilities, funeral homes, colleges and military installations, these helpful, comforting resources can be uniquely presented in *LifeLights* display racks, available from Jewish Lights. **Each *LifeLight* topic is sold in packs of twelve for $9.95.** General discounts are available for quantity purchases.

Visit us online at **www.jewishlights.com** for a complete list of titles, authors, prices and ordering information, or call us at (802) 457-4000 or toll free at (800) 962-4544.

Congregation Resources

Inspired Jewish Leadership: Practical Approaches to Building Strong Communities
By Dr. Erica Brown
6 x 9, 256 pp, HC, 978-1-58023-361-3 **$24.99**

Becoming a Congregation of Learners: Learning as a Key to Revitalizing
Congregational Life *By Isa Aron, PhD; Foreword by Rabbi Lawrence A. Hoffman*
6 x 9, 304 pp, Quality PB, 978-1-58023-089-6 **$19.95**

Finding a Spiritual Home: How a New Generation of Jews Can Transform the
American Synagogue *By Rabbi Sidney Schwarz*
6 x 9, 352 pp, Quality PB, 978-1-58023-185-5 **$19.95**

Jewish Pastoral Care, 2nd Edition: A Practical Handbook from Traditional &
Contemporary Sources *Edited by Rabbi Dayle A. Friedman, MSW, MAJCS, BCC*
6 x 9, 528 pp, HC, 978-1-58023-221-0 **$40.00**

Jewish Spiritual Direction: An Innovative Guide from Traditional and Contemporary
Sources *Edited by Rabbi Howard A. Addison and Barbara Eve Breitman*
6 x 9, 368 pp, HC, 978-1-58023-230-2 **$30.00**

The Self-Renewing Congregation: Organizational Strategies for Revitalizing
Congregational Life *By Isa Aron, PhD; Foreword by Dr. Ron Wolfson*
6 x 9, 304 pp, Quality PB, 978-1-58023-166-4 **$19.95**

Spiritual Community: The Power to Restore Hope, Commitment and Joy
By Rabbi David A. Teutsch, PhD 5½ x 8½, 144 pp, HC, 978-1-58023-270-8 **$19.99**

The Spirituality of Welcoming: How to Transform Your Congregation into a
Sacred Community *By Dr. Ron Wolfson* 6 x 9, 224 pp, Quality PB, 978-1-58023-244-9 **$19.99**

Rethinking Synagogues: A New Vocabulary for Congregational Life
By Rabbi Lawrence A. Hoffman 6 x 9, 240 pp, Quality PB, 978-1-58023-248-7 **$19.99**

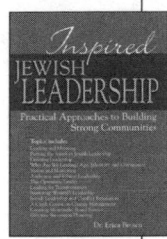

Children's Books

What You Will See Inside a Synagogue
By Rabbi Lawrence A. Hoffman and Dr. Ron Wolfson; Full-color photos by Bill Aron
A colorful, fun-to-read introduction that explains the ways and whys of Jewish
worship and religious life. 8½ x 10½, 32 pp, Full-color photos, Quality PB, 978-1-59473-256-0 **$8.99**
For ages 6 & up (A book from SkyLight Paths, Jewish Lights' sister imprint)

The Kids' Fun Book of Jewish Time
By Emily Sper 9 x 7½, 24 pp, Full-color illus., HC, 978-1-58023-311-8 **$16.99**

In God's Hands
By Lawrence Kushner and Gary Schmidt 9 x 12, 32 pp, HC, 978-1-58023-224-1 **$16.99**

Because Nothing Looks Like God
By Lawrence and Karen Kushner
Introduces children to the possibilities of spiritual life.
11 x 8½, 32 pp, Full-color Illus., HC, 978-1-58023-092-6 **$17.99** *For ages 4 & up*

Board Book Companions to *Because Nothing Looks Like God*
5 x 5, 24 pp, Full-color illus., SkyLight Paths Board Books *For ages 0–4*

What Does God Look Like? 978-1-893361-23-2 **$7.99**
How Does God Make Things Happen? 978-1-893361-24-9 **$7.95**
Where Is God? 978-1-893361-17-1 **$7.99**

The Book of Miracles: A Young Person's Guide to Jewish Spiritual Awareness
By Lawrence Kushner. All-new illustrations by the author
6 x 9, 96 pp, 2-color illus., HC, 978-1-879045-78-1 **$16.95** *For ages 9 and up*

In Our Image: God's First Creatures
By Nancy Sohn Swartz 9 x 12, 32 pp, Full-color illus., HC, 978-1-879045-99-6 **$16.95**
For ages 4 & up

Also Available as a Board Book: **How Did the Animals Help God?**
5 x 5, 24 pp, Board, Full-color illus., 978-1-59473-044-3 **$7.99** *For ages 0–4*
(A book from SkyLight Paths, Jewish Lights' sister imprint)

What Makes Someone a Jew? *By Lauren Seidman*
Reflects the changing face of American Judaism.
10 x 8½, 32 pp, Full-color photos, Quality PB Original, 978-1-58023-321-7 **$8.99** *For ages 3–6*

Children's Books by Sandy Eisenberg Sasso

Adam & Eve's First Sunset: God's New Day
Engaging new story explores fear and hope, faith and gratitude in ways that will delight kids and adults—inspiring us to bless each of God's days and nights.
9 x 12, 32 pp, Full-color illus., HC, 978-1-58023-177-0 **$17.95** *For ages 4 & up*

Also Available as a Board Book: **Adam and Eve's New Day**
5 x 5, 24 pp, Full-color illus., Board, 978-1-59473-205-8 **$7.99** *For ages 0–4*
(A book from SkyLight Paths, Jewish Lights' sister imprint)

But God Remembered
Stories of Women from Creation to the Promised Land
Four different stories of women—Lillith, Serach, Bityah, and the Daughters of Z—teach us important values through their faith and actions.
9 x 12, 32 pp, Full-color illus., Quality PB, 978-1-58023-372-9 **$8.99**; HC, 978-1-879045-43-9 **$16.95** *For ages 8 & up*

Cain & Abel: Finding the Fruits of Peace
Shows children that we have the power to deal with anger in positive ways. Provides questions for kids and adults to explore together.
9 x 12, 32 pp, Full-color illus., HC, 978-1-58023-123-7 **$16.95** *For ages 5 & up*

God in Between
If you wanted to find God, where would you look? This magical, mythical tale teaches that God can be found where we are: within all of us and the relationships between us. 9 x 12, 32 pp, Full-color illus., HC, 978-1-879045-86-6 **$16.95** *For ages 4 & up*

God's Paintbrush: Special 10th Anniversary Edition
Wonderfully interactive, invites children of all faiths and backgrounds to encounter God through moments in their own lives. Provides questions adult and child can explore together. 11 x 8½, 32 pp, Full-color illus., HC, 978-1-58023-195-4 **$17.95** *For ages 4 & up*

Also Available: **God's Paintbrush Teacher's Guide**
8½ x 11, 32 pp, PB, 978-1-879045-57-6 **$8.95**

God's Paintbrush Celebration Kit
A Spiritual Activity Kit for Teachers and Students of All Faiths, All Backgrounds
Additional activity sheets available:
8-Student Activity Sheet Pack (40 sheets/5 sessions), 978-1-58023-058-2 **$19.95**
Single-Student Activity Sheet Pack (5 sessions), 978-1-58023-059-9 **$3.95**

In God's Name
Like an ancient myth in its poetic text and vibrant illustrations, this award-winning modern fable about the search for God's name celebrates the diversity and, at the same time, the unity of all people.
9 x 12, 32 pp, Full-color illus., HC, 978-1-879045-26-2 **$16.99** *For ages 4 & up*

Also Available as a Board Book: **What Is God's Name?**
5 x 5, 24 pp, Board, Full-color illus., 978-1-893361-10-2 **$7.99** *For ages 0–4*
(A book from SkyLight Paths, Jewish Lights' sister imprint)

Also Available: **In God's Name video and study guide**
Computer animation, original music, and children's voices. 18 min. **$29.99**

Also Available in Spanish: **El nombre de Dios**
9 x 12, 32 pp, Full-color illus., HC, 978-1-893361-63-8 **$16.95**
(A book from SkyLight Paths, Jewish Lights' sister imprint)

Noah's Wife: The Story of Naamah
When God tells Noah to bring the animals of the world onto the ark, God also calls on Naamah, Noah's wife, to save each plant on Earth. Based on an ancient text.
9 x 12, 32 pp, Full-color illus., HC, 978-1-58023-134-3 **$16.95** *For ages 4 & up*

Also Available as a Board Book: **Naamah, Noah's Wife**
5 x 5, 24 pp, Full-color illus., Board, 978-1-893361-56-0 **$7.95** *For ages 0–4*
(A book from SkyLight Paths, Jewish Lights' sister imprint)

For Heaven's Sake: Finding God in Unexpected Places
9 x 12, 32 pp, Full-color illus., HC, 978-1-58023-054-4 **$16.95** *For ages 4 & up*

God Said Amen: Finding the Answers to Our Prayers
9 x 12, 32 pp, Full-color illus., HC, 978-1-58023-080-3 **$16.95** *For ages 4 & up*

Meditation

Jewish Meditation Practices for Everyday Life
Awakening Your Heart, Connecting with God
By Rabbi Jeff Roth Offers a fresh take on meditation that draws on life experience and living life with greater clarity as opposed to the traditional method of rigorous study. 6 x 9, 224 pp, Quality PB Original, 978-1-58023-397-2 **$18.99**

The Handbook of Jewish Meditation Practices
A Guide for Enriching the Sabbath and Other Days of Your Life
By Rabbi David A. Cooper Easy-to-learn meditation techniques.
6 x 9, 208 pp, Quality PB, 978-1-58023-102-2 **$16.95**

Discovering Jewish Meditation: Instruction & Guidance for Learning an Ancient Spiritual Practice *By Nan Fink Gefen* 6 x 9, 208 pp, Quality PB, 978-1-58023-067-4 **$16.95**

Meditation from the Heart of Judaism: Today's Teachers Share Their Practices, Techniques, and Faith *Edited by Avram Davis*
6 x 9, 256 pp, Quality PB, 978-1-58023-049-0 **$16.95**

Ritual/Sacred Practice

The Jewish Dream Book: The Key to Opening the Inner Meaning of Your Dreams *By Vanessa L. Ochs with Elizabeth Ochs; Full-color illus. by Kristina Swarner* Instructions for how modern people can perform ancient Jewish dream practices and dream interpretations drawn from the Jewish wisdom tradition.
8 x 8, 128 pp, Full-color illus., Deluxe PB w/flaps, 978-1-58023-132-9 **$16.95**

God in Your Body: Kabbalah, Mindfulness and Embodied Spiritual Practice
By Jay Michaelson
The first comprehensive treatment of the body in Jewish spiritual practice and an essential guide to the sacred.
6 x 9, 288 pp, Quality PB, 978-1-58023-304-0 **$18.99**

The Book of Jewish Sacred Practices: CLAL's Guide to Everyday & Holiday Rituals & Blessings *Edited by Rabbi Irwin Kula and Vanessa L. Ochs, PhD*
6 x 9, 368 pp, Quality PB, 978-1-58023-152-7 **$18.95**

Jewish Ritual: A Brief Introduction for Christians
By Rabbi Kerry M. Olitzky and Rabbi Daniel Judson
5½ x 8½, 144 pp, Quality PB, 978-1-58023-210-4 **$14.99**

The Rituals & Practices of a Jewish Life: A Handbook for Personal Spiritual Renewal *Edited by Rabbi Kerry M. Olitzky and Rabbi Daniel Judson*
6 x 9, 272 pp, illus., Quality PB, 978-1-58023-169-5 **$18.95**

The Sacred Art of Lovingkindness: Preparing to Practice
By Rabbi Rami Shapiro 5½ x 8¼, 176 pp, Quality PB, 978-1-59473-151-8 **$16.99**
(A book from SkyLight Paths, Jewish Lights' sister imprint)

Science Fiction/Mystery & Detective Fiction

Mystery Midrash: An Anthology of Jewish Mystery & Detective Fiction
Edited by Lawrence W. Raphael; Preface by Joel Siegel
6 x 9, 304 pp, Quality PB, 978-1-58023-055-1 **$16.95**

Criminal Kabbalah: An Intriguing Anthology of Jewish Mystery & Detective Fiction *Edited by Lawrence W. Raphael; Foreword by Laurie R. King*
All-new stories from twelve of today's masters of mystery and detective fiction—sure to delight mystery buffs of all faith traditions.
6 x 9, 256 pp, Quality PB, 978-1-58023-109-1 **$16.95**

Wandering Stars: An Anthology of Jewish Fantasy & Science Fiction
Edited by Jack Dann; Introduction by Isaac Asimov
6 x 9, 272 pp, Quality PB, 978-1-58023-005-6 **$18.99**

More Wandering Stars: An Anthology of Outstanding Stories of Jewish Fantasy and Science Fiction *Edited by Jack Dann; Introduction by Isaac Asimov*
6 x 9, 192 pp, Quality PB, 978-1-58023-063-6 **$16.95**

Current Events/History

A Dream of Zion: American Jews Reflect on Why Israel Matters to Them
Edited by Rabbi Jeffrey K. Salkin Explores what Jewish people in America have to say about Israel. 6 x 9, 304 pp, HC, 978-1-58023-340-8 **$24.99**
Also Available: **A Dream of Zion Teacher's Guide** 8½ x 11, 32 pp, PB, 978-1-58023-356-9 **$8.99**

The Jewish Connection to Israel, the Promised Land: A Brief Introduction for Christians *By Rabbi Eugene Korn, PhD* 5½ x 8½, 192 pp, Quality PB, 978-1-58023-318-7 **$14.99**

The Story of the Jews: A 4,000-Year Adventure—A Graphic History Book
Written & illustrated by Stan Mack 6 x 9, 288 pp, illus., Quality PB, 978-1-58023-155-8 **$16.99**

Hannah Senesh: Her Life and Diary, the First Complete Edition
By Hannah Senesh; Foreword by Marge Piercy; Preface by Eitan Senesh; Afterword by Roberta Grossman
6 x 9, 368 pp, b/w photos, Quality PB, 978-1-58023-342-2 **$19.99**

The Ethiopian Jews of Israel: Personal Stories of Life in the Promised Land *By Len Lyons, PhD; Foreword by Alan Dershowitz; Photographs by Ilan Ossendryver* Recounts, through photographs and words, stories of Ethiopian Jews.
10½ x 10, 240 pp, 100 full-color photos, HC, 978-1-58023-323-1 **$34.99**

Foundations of Sephardic Spirituality: The Inner Life of Jews of the Ottoman Empire
By Rabbi Marc D. Angel, PhD 6 x 9, 224 pp, Quality PB, 978-1-58023-341-5 **$18.99**

Judaism and Justice: The Jewish Passion to Repair the World
By Rabbi Sidney Schwarz 6 x 9, 352 pp, Quality PB, 978-1-58023-353-8 **$19.99**

Ecology/Environment

A Wild Faith: Jewish Ways into Wilderness, Wilderness Ways into Judaism
By Rabbi Mike Comins; Foreword by Nigel Savage
Offers ways to enliven and deepen your spiritual life through wilderness experience.
6 x 9, 240 pp, Quality PB, 978-1-58023-316-3 **$16.99**

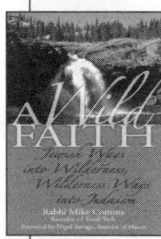

Ecology & the Jewish Spirit: Where Nature & the Sacred Meet
Edited by Ellen Bernstein 6 x 9, 288 pp, Quality PB, 978-1-58023-082-7 **$18.99**

Torah of the Earth: Exploring 4,000 Years of Ecology in Jewish Thought
Vol. 1: Biblical Israel: One Land, One People; Rabbinic Judaism: One People, Many Lands
Vol. 2: Zionism: One Land, Two Peoples; Eco-Judaism: One Earth, Many Peoples
Edited by Arthur Waskow Vol. 1: 6 x 9, 272 pp, Quality PB, 978-1-58023-086-5 **$19.95**
Vol. 2: 6 x 9, 336 pp, Quality PB, 978-1-58023-087-2 **$19.95**

The Way Into Judaism and the Environment *By Jeremy Benstein, PhD*
6 x 9, 288 pp, Quality PB, 978-1-58023-368-2 **$18.99**; HC, 978-1-58023-268-5 **$24.99**

Grief/Healing

Healing and the Jewish Imagination: Spiritual and Practical Perspectives on Judaism and Health *Edited by Rabbi William Cutter, PhD* Explores Judaism for comfort in times of illness and perspectives on suffering.
6 x 9, 240 pp, Quality PB, 978-1-58023-373-6 **$19.99**; HC, 978-1-58023-314-9 **$24.99**

Grief in Our Seasons: A Mourner's Kaddish Companion *By Rabbi Kerry M. Olitzky*
4½ x 6½, 448 pp, Quality PB, 978-1-879045-55-2 **$15.95**

Healing of Soul, Healing of Body: Spiritual Leaders Unfold the Strength & Solace in Psalms *Edited by Rabbi Simkha Y. Weintraub, CSW*
6 x 9, 128 pp, 2-color illus. text, Quality PB, 978-1-879045-31-6 **$14.99**

Mourning & Mitzvah, 2nd Edition: A Guided Journal for Walking the Mourner's Path through Grief to Healing *By Anne Brener, LCSW*
7½ x 9, 304 pp, Quality PB, 978-1-58023-113-8 **$19.99**

Tears of Sorrow, Seeds of Hope, 2nd Edition: A Jewish Spiritual Companion for Infertility and Pregnancy Loss *By Rabbi Nina Beth Cardin*
6 x 9, 208 pp, Quality PB, 978-1-58023-233-3 **$18.99**

A Time to Mourn, a Time to Comfort, 2nd Edition: A Guide to Jewish Bereavement *By Dr. Ron Wolfson*
7 x 9, 384 pp, Quality PB, 978-1-58023-253-1 **$19.99**

When a Grandparent Dies: A Kid's Own Remembering Workbook for Dealing with Shiva and the Year Beyond *By Nechama Liss-Levinson, PhD*
8 x 10, 48 pp, 2-color text, HC, 978-1-879045-44-6 **$15.95** *For ages 7–13*

Judaism / Christianity / Interfaith

Talking about God: Exploring the Meaning of Religious Life with Kierkegaard, Buber, Tillich and Heschel *by Daniel F. Polish, PhD*
Examines the meaning of the human religious experience with the greatest theologians of modern times. 6 x 9, 176 pp, HC, 978-1-59473-230-0 **$21.99**
(A book from SkyLight Paths, Jewish Lights' sister imprint)

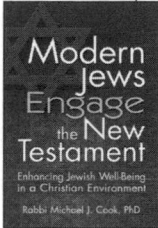

Interactive Faith: The Essential Interreligious Community-Building Handbook
Edited by Rev. Bud Heckman with Rori Picker Neiss
A guide to the key methods and resources of the interfaith movement.
6 x 9, 320 pp, HC, 978-1-59473-237-9 **$29.99**
(A book from SkyLight Paths, Jewish Lights' sister imprint)

The Jewish Approach to Repairing the World (*Tikkun Olam*)
A Brief Introduction for Christians *by Rabbi Elliot N. Dorff, PhD, with Reverend Cory Willson*
A window into the Jewish idea of responsibility to care for the world.
5½ x 8½, 256 pp, Quality PB, 978-1-58023-349-1 **$16.99**

Modern Jews Engage the New Testament: Enhancing Jewish Well-Being in a Christian Environment *by Rabbi Michael J. Cook, PhD*
A look at the dynamics of the New Testament.
6 x 9, 416 pp, HC, 978-1-58023-313-2 **$29.99**

Disaster Spiritual Care: Practical Clergy Responses to Community, Regional and National Tragedy
Edited by Rabbi Stephen B. Roberts, BCJC, & Rev. Willard W.C. Ashley, Sr., DMin, DH
The definitive reference for pastoral caregivers of all faiths involved in disaster response.
6 x 9, 384 pp, HC, 978-1-59473-240-9 **$40.00** *(A book from SkyLight Paths, Jewish Lights' sister imprint)*

The Changing Christian World: A Brief Introduction for Jews
by Rabbi Leonard A. Schoolman 5½ x 8½, 176 pp, Quality PB, 978-1-58023-344-6 **$16.99**

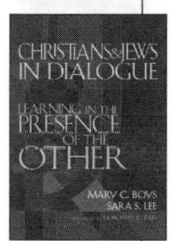

The Jewish Connection to Israel, the Promised Land: A Brief Introduction for Christians *by Rabbi Eugene Korn, PhD* 5½ x 8½, 192 pp, Quality PB, 978-1-58023-318-7 **$14.99**

Christians and Jews in Dialogue: Learning in the Presence of the Other
by Mary C. Boys and Sara S. Lee; Foreword by Dorothy C. Bass
Inspires renewed commitment to dialogue between religious traditions.
6 x 9, 240 pp, Quality PB, 978-1-59473-254-6 **$18.99**; HC, 978-1-59473-144-0 **$21.99**
(A book from SkyLight Paths, Jewish Lights' sister imprint)

Healing the Jewish-Christian Rift: Growing Beyond Our Wounded History
by Ron Miller and Laura Bernstein; Foreword by Dr. Beatrice Bruteau
6 x 9, 288 pp, Quality PB, 978-1-59473-139-6 **$18.99**
(A book from SkyLight Paths, Jewish Lights' sister imprint)

Introducing My Faith and My Community
The Jewish Outreach Institute Guide for the Christian in a Jewish Interfaith Relationship
by Rabbi Kerry M. Olitzky 6 x 9, 176 pp, Quality PB, 978-1-58023-192-3 **$16.99**

The Jewish Approach to God: A Brief Introduction for Christians
by Rabbi Neil Gillman 5½ x 8½, 192 pp, Quality PB, Original 978-1-58023-190-9 **$16.95**

Jewish Holidays: A Brief Introduction for Christians *by Rabbi Kerry M. Olitzky and Rabbi Daniel Judson* 5½ x 8½, 176 pp, Quality PB Original, 978-1-58023-302-6 **$16.99**

Jewish Ritual: A Brief Introduction for Christians *by Rabbi Kerry M. Olitzky and Rabbi Daniel Judson* 5½ x 8½, 144 pp, Quality PB Original, 978-1-58023-210-4 **$14.99**

Jewish Spirituality: A Brief Introduction for Christians *by Rabbi Lawrence Kushner*
5½ x 8½, 112 pp, Quality PB Original, 978-1-58023-150-3 **$12.95**

A Jewish Understanding of the New Testament
by Rabbi Samuel Sandmel; new Preface by Rabbi David Sandmel 5½ x 8½, 368 pp, Quality PB,
978-1-59473-048-1 **$19.99** *(A book from SkyLight Paths, Jewish Lights' sister imprint)*

We Jews and Jesus: Exploring Theological Differences for Mutual Understanding
by Rabbi Samuel Sandmel; new Preface by Rabbi David Sandmel A Classic Reprint
6 x 9, 192 pp, Quality PB, 978-1-59473-208-9 **$16.99**
(A book from SkyLight Paths, Jewish Lights' sister imprint)

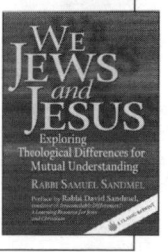

Show Me Your Way: The Complete Guide to Exploring Interfaith Spiritual Direction
by Howard A. Addison 5½ x 8½, 240 pp, Quality PB, 978-1-893361-41-6 **$16.95**
(A book from SkyLight Paths, Jewish Lights' sister imprint)

Theology/Philosophy/The Way Into... Series

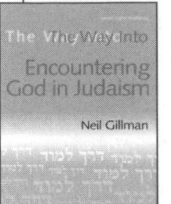

The Way Into... series offers an accessible and highly usable "guided tour" of the Jewish faith, people, history and beliefs—in total, an introduction to Judaism that will enable you to understand and interact with the sacred texts of the Jewish tradition. Each volume is written by a leading contemporary scholar and teacher, and explores one key aspect of Judaism. *The Way Into...* series enables all readers to achieve a real sense of Jewish cultural literacy through guided study.

The Way Into Encountering God in Judaism
By Rabbi Neil Gillman, PhD
For everyone who wants to understand how Jews have encountered God throughout history and today.
6 x 9, 240 pp, Quality PB, 978-1-58023-199-2 **$18.99**; HC, 978-1-58023-025-4 **$21.95**
Also Available: **The Jewish Approach to God:** A Brief Introduction for Christians
By Rabbi Neil Gillman, PhD
5½ x 8½, 192 pp, Quality PB, 978-1-58023-190-9 **$16.95**

The Way Into Jewish Mystical Tradition
By Rabbi Lawrence Kushner
Allows readers to interact directly with the sacred mystical text of the Jewish tradition. An accessible introduction to the concepts of Jewish mysticism, their religious and spiritual significance and how they relate to life today.
6 x 9, 224 pp, Quality PB, 978-1-58023-200-5 **$18.99**; HC, 978-1-58023-029-2 **$21.95**

The Way Into Jewish Prayer
By Rabbi Lawrence A. Hoffman, PhD
Opens the door to 3,000 years of Jewish prayer, making available all anyone needs to feel at home in the Jewish way of communicating with God.
6 x 9, 208 pp, Quality PB, 978-1-58023-201-2 **$18.99**

Also Available: **The Way Into Jewish Prayer Teacher's Guide**
By Rabbi Jennifer Ossakow Goldsmith
8½ x 11, 42 pp, Quality PB, 978-1-58023-345-3 **$8.99**
Visit our website to download a free copy.

The Way Into Judaism and the Environment
By Jeremy Benstein, PhD
Explores the ways in which Judaism contributes to contemporary social-environmental issues, the extent to which Judaism is part of the problem and how it can be part of the solution.
6 x 9, 288 pp, Quality PB, 978-1-58023-368-2 **$18.99**; HC, 978-1-58023-268-5 **$24.99**

The Way Into Tikkun Olam (Repairing the World)
By Rabbi Elliot N. Dorff, PhD
An accessible introduction to the Jewish concept of the individual's responsibility to care for others and repair the world.
6 x 9, 304 pp, Quality PB, 978-1-58023-328-6 **$18.99**; 320 pp, HC, 978-1-58023-269-2 **$24.99**

The Way Into Torah
By Rabbi Norman J. Cohen, PhD
Helps guide in the exploration of the origins and development of Torah, explains why it should be studied and how to do it.
6 x 9, 176 pp, Quality PB, 978-1-58023-198-5 **$16.99**

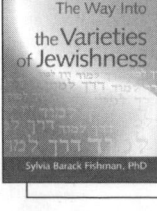

The Way Into the Varieties of Jewishness
By Sylvia Barack Fishman, PhD
Explores the religious and historical understanding of what it has meant to be Jewish from ancient times to the present controversy over "Who is a Jew?"
6 x 9, 288 pp, Quality PB, 978-1-58023-367-5 **$18.99**; HC, 978-1-58023-030-8 **$24.99**

Theology/Philosophy

A Touch of the Sacred: A Theologian's Informal Guide to Jewish Belief
By Dr. Eugene B. Borowitz and Frances W. Schwartz Explores the musings from the leading theologian of liberal Judaism. 6 x 9, 256 pp, HC, 978-1-58023-337-8 **$21.99**

Talking about God: Exploring the Meaning of Religious Life with Kierkegaard, Buber, Tillich and Heschel *By Daniel F. Polish, PhD*
Examines the meaning of the human religious experience with the greatest theologians of modern times. 6 x 9, 160 pp, HC, 978-1-59473-230-0 **$21.99**
(A book from SkyLight Paths, Jewish Lights' sister imprint)

Jews & Judaism in the 21st Century: Human Responsibility, the Presence of God, and the Future of the Covenant *Edited by Rabbi Edward Feinstein; Foreword by Paula E. Hyman* Five celebrated leaders in Judaism examine contemporary Jewish life. 6 x 9, 192 pp, Quality PB, 978-1-58023-374-3 **$19.99**; HC, 978-1-58023-315-6 **$24.99**

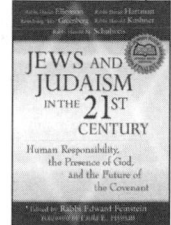

Christians and Jews in Dialogue: Learning in the Presence of the Other
By Mary C. Boys and Sara S. Lee; Foreword by Dr. Dorothy Bass
6 x 9, 240 pp, Quality PB, 978-1-59473-254-6 **$18.99**; HC, 978-1-59473-144-0 **$21.99**
(A book from SkyLight Paths, Jewish Lights' sister imprint)

The Death of Death: Resurrection and Immortality in Jewish Thought
By Neil Gillman 6 x 9, 336 pp, Quality PB, 978-1-58023-081-0 **$18.95**

Ethics of the Sages: Pirke Avot—Annotated & Explained
Translation & Annotation by Rabbi Rami Shapiro
5½ x 8½, 208 pp, Quality PB, 978-1-59473-207-2 **$16.99** *(A book from SkyLight Paths, Jewish Lights' sister imprint)*

Hasidic Tales: Annotated & Explained *By Rabbi Rami Shapiro; Foreword by Andrew Harvey*
5½ x 8½, 240 pp, Quality PB, 978-1-893361-86-7 **$16.95**
(A book from SkyLight Paths, Jewish Lights' sister imprint)

A Heart of Many Rooms: Celebrating the Many Voices within Judaism
By David Hartman 6 x 9, 352 pp, Quality PB, 978-1-58023-156-5 **$19.95**

The Hebrew Prophets: Selections Annotated & Explained
Translation & Annotation by Rabbi Rami Shapiro; Foreword by Zalman M. Schachter-Shalomi
5½ x 8½, 224 pp, Quality PB, 978-1-59473-037-5 **$16.99** *(A book from SkyLight Paths, Jewish Lights' sister imprint)*

A Jewish Understanding of the New Testament
By Rabbi Samuel Sandmel; Preface by Rabbi David Sandmel
5½ x 8½, 368 pp, Quality PB, 978-1-59473-048-1 **$19.99** *(A book from SkyLight Paths, Jewish Lights' sister imprint)*

Keeping Faith with the Psalms: Deepen Your Relationship with God Using the Book of Psalms *By Daniel F. Polish* 6 x 9, 320 pp, Quality PB, 978-1-58023-300-2 **$18.99**

A Living Covenant: The Innovative Spirit in Traditional Judaism
By David Hartman 6 x 9, 368 pp, Quality PB, 978-1-58023-011-7 **$20.00**

Love and Terror in the God Encounter: The Theological Legacy of Rabbi Joseph B. Soloveitchik *By David Hartman* 6 x 9, 240 pp, Quality PB, 978-1-58023-176-3 **$19.95**

The Personhood of God: Biblical Theology, Human Faith and the Divine Image
By Dr. Yochanan Muffs; Foreword by Dr. David Hartman
6 x 9, 240 pp, Quality PB, 978-1-58023-338-5 **$18.99**; HC, 978-1-58023-265-4 **$24.99**

Traces of God: Seeing God in Torah, History and Everyday Life *By Neil Gillman*
6 x 9, 240 pp, Quality PB, 978-1-58023-369-9 **$16.99**; HC, 978-1-58023-249-4 **$21.99**

We Jews and Jesus: Exploring Theological Differences for Mutual Understanding
By Rabbi Samuel Sandmel; Preface by Rabbi David Sandmel
6 x 9, 176 pp, Quality PB, 978-1-59473-208-9 **$16.99** *(A book from SkyLight Paths, Jewish Lights' sister imprint)*

Your Word Is Fire: The Hasidic Masters on Contemplative Prayer
Edited and translated by Arthur Green and Barry W. Holtz
6 x 9, 160 pp, Quality PB, 978-1-879045-25-5 **$15.95**

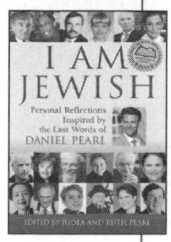

I Am Jewish
Personal Reflections Inspired by the Last Words of Daniel Pearl
Almost 150 Jews—both famous and not—from all walks of life, from all around the world, write about many aspects of their Judaism.
Edited by Judea and Ruth Pearl 6 x 9, 304 pp, Deluxe PB w/flaps, 978-1-58023-259-3 **$18.99**
Download a free copy of the *I Am Jewish Teacher's Guide* at our website:
www.jewishlights.com

Holidays/Holy Days

Rosh Hashanah Readings: Inspiration, Information and Contemplation
Yom Kippur Readings: Inspiration, Information and Contemplation
Edited by Rabbi Dov Peretz Elkins with Section Introductions from Arthur Green's These Are the Words
An extraordinary collection of readings, prayers and insights that enable the modern worshiper to enter into the spirit of the High Holy Days in a personal and powerful way, permitting the meaning of the Jewish New Year to enter the heart.
RHR: 6 x 9, 400 pp, HC, 978-1-58023-239-5 **$24.99**
YKR: 6 x 9, 368 pp, HC, 978-1-58023-271-5 **$24.99**

Jewish Holidays: A Brief Introduction for Christians
By Rabbi Kerry M. Olitzky and Rabbi Daniel Judson
5½ x 8½, 144 pp, Quality PB, 978-1-58023-302-6 **$16.99**

Reclaiming Judaism as a Spiritual Practice: Holy Days and Shabbat
By Rabbi Goldie Milgram
7 x 9, 272 pp, Quality PB, 978-1-58023-205-0 **$19.99**

7th Heaven: Celebrating Shabbat with Rebbe Nachman of Breslov
By Moshe Mykoff with the Breslov Research Institute
5⅛ x 8¼, 224 pp, Deluxe PB w/flaps, 978-1-58023-175-6 **$18.95**

Shabbat, 2nd Edition: The Family Guide to Preparing for and Celebrating the Sabbath
By Dr. Ron Wolfson 7 x 9, 320 pp, illus., Quality PB, 978-1-58023-164-0 **$19.99**

Hanukkah, 2nd Edition: The Family Guide to Spiritual Celebration
By Dr. Ron Wolfson. Edited by Joel Lurie Grishaver.
7 x 9, 240 pp, illus., Quality PB, 978-1-58023-122-0 **$18.95**

The Jewish Family Fun Book, 2nd Edition: Holiday Projects, Everyday Activities, and Travel Ideas with Jewish Themes *By Danielle Dardashti and Roni Sarig. Illus. by Avi Katz.*
6 x 9, 304 pp, 70+ b/w illus. & diagrams, Quality PB, 978-1-58023-333-0 **$18.99**

The Jewish Lights Book of Fun Classroom Activities: Simple and Seasonal Projects for Teachers and Students *By Danielle Dardashti and Roni Sarig*
6 x 9, 240 pp, Quality PB, 978-1-58023-206-7 **$19.99**

Passover

My People's Passover Haggadah
Traditional Texts, Modern Commentaries
Edited by Rabbi Lawrence A. Hoffman, PhD, and David Arnow, PhD
A diverse and exciting collection of commentaries on the traditional Passover Haggadah—in two volumes!
Vol. 1: 7 x 10, 304 pp, HC, 978-1-58023-354-5 **$24.99**
Vol. 2: 7 x 10, 320 pp, HC, 978-1-58023-346-0 **$24.99**

Leading the Passover Journey
The Seder's Meaning Revealed, the Haggadah's Story Retold
By Rabbi Nathan Laufer
Uncovers the hidden meaning of the Seder's rituals and customs.
6 x 9, 224 pp, Quality PB, 978-1-58023-399-6 **$18.99**; HC, 978-1-58023-211-1 **$24.99**

The Women's Passover Companion: Women's Reflections on the Festival of Freedom
Edited by Rabbi Sharon Cohen Anisfeld, Tara Mohr, and Catherine Spector
6 x 9, 352 pp, Quality PB, 978-1-58023-231-9 **$19.99**

The Women's Seder Sourcebook: Rituals & Readings for Use at the Passover Seder
Edited by Rabbi Sharon Cohen Anisfeld, Tara Mohr, and Catherine Spector
6 x 9, 384 pp, Quality PB, 978-1-58023-232-6 **$19.99**

Creating Lively Passover Seders: A Sourcebook of Engaging Tales, Texts & Activities
By David Arnow, PhD 7 x 9, 416 pp, Quality PB, 978-1-58023-184-8 **$24.99**

Passover, 2nd Edition: The Family Guide to Spiritual Celebration
By Dr. Ron Wolfson with Joel Lurie Grishaver 7 x 9, 352 pp, Quality PB, 978-1-58023-174-9 **$19.95**

Life Cycle
Marriage / Parenting / Family / Aging

The New Jewish Baby Album: Creating and Celebrating the Beginning of a Spiritual Life—A Jewish Lights Companion
By the Editors at Jewish Lights. Foreword by Anita Diamant. Preface by Rabbi Sandy Eisenberg Sasso.
A spiritual keepsake that will be treasured for generations. More than just a memory book, *shows you how—and why it's important*—to create a Jewish home and a Jewish life. 8 x 10, 64 pp, Deluxe Padded HC, Full-color illus., 978-1-58023-138-1 **$19.95**

The Jewish Pregnancy Book: A Resource for the Soul, Body & Mind during Pregnancy, Birth & the First Three Months
By Sandy Falk, MD, and Rabbi Daniel Judson, with Steven A. Rapp
Includes medical information, prayers and rituals for each stage of pregnancy, from a liberal Jewish perspective. 7 x 10, 208 pp, Quality PB, b/w photos, 978-1-58023-178-7 **$16.95**

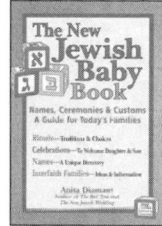

Celebrating Your New Jewish Daughter: Creating Jewish Ways to Welcome Baby Girls into the Covenant—New and Traditional Ceremonies *By Debra Nussbaum Cohen; Foreword by Rabbi Sandy Eisenberg Sasso* 6 x 9, 272 pp, Quality PB, 978-1-58023-090-2 **$18.95**

The New Jewish Baby Book, 2nd Edition: Names, Ceremonies & Customs—A Guide for Today's Families *By Anita Diamant* 6 x 9, 336 pp, Quality PB, 978-1-58023-251-7 **$19.99**

Parenting as a Spiritual Journey: Deepening Ordinary and Extraordinary Events into Sacred Occasions *By Rabbi Nancy Fuchs-Kreimer*
6 x 9, 224 pp, Quality PB, 978-1-58023-016-2 **$16.95**

Parenting Jewish Teens: A Guide for the Perplexed
By Joanne Doades
Explores the questions and issues that shape the world in which today's Jewish teenagers live.
6 x 9, 200 pp, Quality PB, 978-1-58023-305-7 **$16.99**

Judaism for Two: A Spiritual Guide for Strengthening and Celebrating Your Loving Relationship *By Rabbi Nancy Fuchs-Kreimer and Rabbi Nancy H. Wiener; Foreword by Rabbi Elliot N. Dorff* Addresses the ways Jewish teachings can enhance and strengthen committed relationships. 6 x 9, 224 pp, Quality PB, 978-1-58023-254-8 **$16.99**

Embracing the Covenant: Converts to Judaism Talk About Why & How
By Rabbi Allan Berkowitz and Patti Moskovitz 6 x 9, 192 pp, Quality PB, 978-1-879045-50-7 **$16.95**

The Guide to Jewish Interfaith Family Life: An InterfaithFamily.com Handbook
Edited by Ronnie Friedland and Edmund Case 6 x 9, 384 pp, Quality PB, 978-1-58023-153-4 **$18.95**

Introducing My Faith and My Community
The Jewish Outreach Institute Guide for the Christian in a Jewish Interfaith Relationship
By Rabbi Kerry M. Olitzky 6 x 9, 176 pp, Quality PB, 978-1-58023-192-3 **$16.99**

Making a Successful Jewish Interfaith Marriage: The Jewish Outreach Institute Guide to Opportunities, Challenges and Resources *By Rabbi Kerry M. Olitzky with Joan Peterson Littman*
6 x 9, 176 pp, Quality PB, 978-1-58023-170-1 **$16.95**

The Creative Jewish Wedding Book, 2nd Edition: A Hands-On Guide to New & Old Traditions, Ceremonies & Celebrations *By Gabrielle Kaplan-Mayer*
9 x 9, 288 pp, b/w photos, Quality PB, 978-1-58023-398-9 **$19.99**

Divorce Is a Mitzvah: A Practical Guide to Finding Wholeness and Holiness When Your Marriage Dies *By Rabbi Perry Netter; Afterword by Rabbi Laura Geller.*
6 x 9, 224 pp, Quality PB, 978-1-58023-172-5 **$16.95**

A Heart of Wisdom: Making the Jewish Journey from Midlife through the Elder Years
Edited by Susan Berrin; Foreword by Harold Kushner
6 x 9, 384 pp, Quality PB, 978-1-58023-051-3 **$18.95**

So That Your Values Live On: Ethical Wills and How to Prepare Them
Edited by Jack Riemer and Nathaniel Stampfer
6 x 9, 272 pp, Quality PB, 978-1-879045-34-7 **$18.99**

Spirituality/Lawrence Kushner

Filling Words with Light: Hasidic and Mystical Reflections on Jewish Prayer
By Lawrence Kushner and Nehemia Polen
5½ x 8½, 176 pp, Quality PB, 978-1-58023-238-8 **$16.99**; HC, 978-1-58023-216-6 **$21.99**

The Book of Letters: A Mystical Hebrew Alphabet
Popular HC Edition, 6 x 9, 80 pp, 2-color text, 978-1-879045-00-2 **$24.95**
Collector's Limited Edition, 9 x 12, 80 pp, gold foil embossed pages, w/limited edition silkscreened print, 978-1-879045-04-0 **$349.00**

The Book of Miracles: A Young Person's Guide to Jewish Spiritual Awareness
6 x 9, 96 pp, 2-color illus., HC, 978-1-879045-78-1 **$16.95** *For ages 9 and up*

The Book of Words: Talking Spiritual Life, Living Spiritual Talk
6 x 9, 160 pp, Quality PB, 978-1-58023-020-9 **$16.95**

Eyes Remade for Wonder: A Lawrence Kushner Reader *Introduction by Thomas Moore*
6 x 9, 240 pp, Quality PB, 978-1-58023-042-1 **$18.95**

God Was in This Place & I, i Did Not Know: Finding Self, Spirituality and Ultimate Meaning 6 x 9, 192 pp, Quality PB, 978-1-879045-33-0 **$16.95**

Honey from the Rock: An Introduction to Jewish Mysticism
6 x 9, 176 pp, Quality PB, 978-1-58023-073-5 **$16.95**

Invisible Lines of Connection: Sacred Stories of the Ordinary
5½ x 8½, 160 pp, Quality PB, 978-1-879045-98-9 **$15.95**

Jewish Spirituality—A Brief Introduction for Christians
5½ x 8½, 112 pp, Quality PB, 978-1-58023-150-3 **$12.95**

The River of Light: Jewish Mystical Awareness
6 x 9, 192 pp, Quality PB, 978-1-58023-096-4 **$16.95**

The Way Into Jewish Mystical Tradition
6 x 9, 224 pp, Quality PB, 978-1-58023-200-5 **$18.99**; HC, 978-1-58023-029-2 **$21.95**

Spirituality/Prayer

My People's Passover Haggadah: Traditional Texts, Modern Commentaries
Edited by Rabbi Lawrence A. Hoffman, PhD, and David Arnow, PhD Diverse commentaries on the traditional Passover Haggadah—in two volumes! Vol. 1: 7 x 10, 304 pp, HC 978-1-58023-354-5 **$24.99** Vol. 2: 7 x 10, 320 pp, HC, 978-1-58023-346-0 **$24.99**

Witnesses to the One: The Spiritual History of the *Sh'ma By Rabbi Joseph B. Meszler; Foreword by Rabbi Elyse Goldstein* 6 x 9, 176 pp, HC, 978-1-58023-309-5 **$19.99**

My People's Prayer Book Series

Traditional Prayers, Modern Commentaries *Edited by Rabbi Lawrence A. Hoffman* Provides diverse and exciting commentary to the traditional liturgy, helping modern men and women find new wisdom in Jewish prayer, and bring liturgy into their lives. Each book includes Hebrew text, modern translation, and commentaries from all perspectives of the Jewish world.

Vol. 1—The *Sh'ma* and Its Blessings
7 x 10, 168 pp, HC, 978-1-879045-79-8 **$24.99**
Vol. 2—The *Amidah*
7 x 10, 240 pp, HC, 978-1-879045-80-4 **$24.95**
Vol. 3—*P'sukei D'zimrah* (Morning Psalms)
7 x 10, 240 pp, HC, 978-1-879045-81-1 **$24.95**
Vol. 4—*Seder K'riat Hatorah* (The Torah Service)
7 x 10, 264 pp, HC, 978-1-879045-82-8 **$23.95**
Vol. 5—*Birkhot Hashachar* (Morning Blessings)
7 x 10, 240 pp, HC, 978-1-879045-83-5 **$24.95**
Vol. 6—*Tachanun* and Concluding Prayers
7 x 10, 240 pp, HC, 978-1-879045-84-2 **$24.95**
Vol. 7—Shabbat at Home
7 x 10, 240 pp, HC, 978-1-879045-85-9 **$24.95**
Vol. 8—*Kabbalat Shabbat* (Welcoming Shabbat in the Synagogue)
7 x 10, 240 pp, HC, 978-1-58023-121-3 **$24.99**
Vol. 9—Welcoming the Night: *Minchah* and *Ma'ariv* (Afternoon and Evening Prayer) 7 x 10, 272 pp, HC, 978-1-58023-262-3 **$24.99**
Vol. 10—Shabbat Morning: *Shacharit* and *Musaf* (Morning and Additional Services) 7 x 10, 240 pp, HC, 978-1-58023-240-1 **$24.99**

Spirituality

Journeys to a Jewish Life: Inspiring Stories from the Spiritual Journeys of American Jews *By Paula Amann*
Examines the soul treks of Jews lost and found. 6 x 9, 208 pp, HC, 978-1-58023-317-0 **$19.99**

The Adventures of Rabbi Harvey: A Graphic Novel of Jewish Wisdom and Wit in the Wild West *By Steve Sheinkin*
Jewish and American folktales combine in this witty and original graphic novel collection. Creatively retold and set on the western frontier of the 1870s.
6 x 9, 144 pp, Full-color illus., Quality PB, 978-1-58023-310-1 **$16.99**

Rabbi Harvey Rides Again
A Graphic Novel of Jewish Folktales Let Loose in the Wild West *By Steve Sheinkin*
6 x 9, 144 pp, Quality PB Original, Full-color illus., 978-1-58023-347-7 **$16.99**

Ethics of the Sages: Pirke Avot—Annotated & Explained
Translation and Annotation by Rabbi Rami Shapiro 5½ x 8½, 192 pp, Quality PB, 978-1-59473-207-2
$16.99 *(A book from SkyLight Paths, Jewish Lights' sister imprint)*

A Book of Life: Embracing Judaism as a Spiritual Practice
By Michael Strassfeld 6 x 9, 528 pp, Quality PB, 978-1-58023-247-0 **$19.99**

Meaning and Mitzvah: Daily Practices for Reclaiming Judaism through Prayer, God, Torah, Hebrew, Mitzvot and Peoplehood *By Rabbi Goldie Milgram*
7 x 9, 336 pp, Quality PB, 978-1-58023-256-2 **$19.99**

The Soul of the Story: Meetings with Remarkable People
By Rabbi David Zeller 6 x 9, 288 pp, HC, 978-1-58023-272-2 **$21.99**

Aleph-Bet Yoga: Embodying the Hebrew Letters for Physical and Spiritual Well-Being
By Steven A. Rapp. Foreword by Tamar Frankiel, PhD and Judy Greenfeld. Preface by Hart Lazer.
7 x 10, 128 pp, b/w photos, Quality PB, Layflat binding, 978-1-58023-162-6 **$16.95**

Does the Soul Survive? A Jewish Journey to Belief in Afterlife, Past Lives & Living with Purpose *By Rabbi Elie Kaplan Spitz; Foreword by Brian L. Weiss, MD*
6 x 9, 288 pp, Quality PB, 978-1-58023-165-7 **$16.99**

First Steps to a New Jewish Spirit: Reb Zalman's Guide to Recapturing the Intimacy & Ecstasy in Your Relationship with God *By Rabbi Zalman M. Schachter-Shalomi with Donald Gropman* 6 x 9, 144 pp, Quality PB, 978-1-58023-182-4 **$16.95**

God in Our Relationships: Spirituality between People from the Teachings of Martin Buber *By Rabbi Dennis S. Ross* 5½ x 8½, 160 pp, Quality PB, 978-1-58023-147-3 **$16.95**

Judaism, Physics and God: Searching for Sacred Metaphors in a Post-Einstein World
By Rabbi David W. Nelson 6 x 9, 368 pp, Quality PB, inc. reader's discussion guide, 978-1-58023-306-4 **$18.99**;
HC, 352 pp, 978-1-58023-252-4 **$24.99**

The Jewish Lights Spirituality Handbook: A Guide to Understanding, Exploring & Living a Spiritual Life *Edited by Stuart M. Matlins*
What exactly is "Jewish" about spirituality? How do I make it a part of my life? Fifty of today's foremost spiritual leaders share their ideas and experience with us.
6 x 9, 456 pp, Quality PB, 978-1-58023-093-3 **$19.99**

Bringing the Psalms to Life: How to Understand and Use the Book of Psalms
By Daniel F. Polish 6 x 9, 208 pp, Quality PB, 978-1-58023-157-2 **$16.95**;
HC, 978-1-58023-077-3 **$21.95**

God & the Big Bang: Discovering Harmony between Science & Spirituality
By Daniel C. Matt 6 x 9, 216 pp, Quality PB, 978-1-879045-89-7 **$16.99**

Minding the Temple of the Soul: Balancing Body, Mind, and Spirit through Traditional Jewish Prayer, Movement, and Meditation *By Tamar Frankiel, PhD, and Judy Greenfeld*
7 x 10, 184 pp, illus., Quality PB, 978-1-879045-64-4 **$16.95**

One God Clapping: The Spiritual Path of a Zen Rabbi *By Alan Lew with Sherril Jaffe*
5½ x 8½, 336 pp, Quality PB, 978-1-58023-115-2 **$16.95**

There Is No Messiah ... and You're It: The Stunning Transformation of Judaism's Most Provocative Idea *By Rabbi Robert N. Levine, DD*
6 x 9, 192 pp, Quality PB, 978-1-58023-255-5 **$16.99**

These Are the Words: A Vocabulary of Jewish Spiritual Life
By Arthur Green 6 x 9, 304 pp, Quality PB, 978-1-58023-107-7 **$18.95**

Social Justice

Conscience: The Duty to Obey and the Duty to Disobey
By Rabbi Harold M. Schulweis
This clarion call to rethink our moral and political behavior examines the idea of conscience and the role conscience plays in our relationships to governments, law, ethics, religion, human nature, God—and to each other.
6 x 9, 160 pp, HC, 978-1-58023-375-0 **$19.99**

Judaism and Justice: The Jewish Passion to Repair the World
By Rabbi Sidney Schwarz; Foreword by Ruth Messinger
Explores the relationship between Judaism, social justice and the Jewish identity of American Jews, offering new ways to understand these important aspects of Jewish life.
6 x 9, 352 pp, Quality PB, 978-1-58023-353-8 **$19.99**; HC, 978-1-58023-312-5 **$24.99**

Shared Dreams: Martin Luther King, Jr. & the Jewish Community
By Rabbi Marc Schneier; Preface by Martin Luther King III
6 x 9, 240 pp, Quality PB, 978-1-58023-273-9 **$18.99**

Spiritual Activism: A Jewish Guide to Leadership and Repairing the World
By Rabbi Avraham Weiss; Foreword by Alan M. Dershowitz
6 x 9, 224 pp, HC, 978-1-58023-355-2 **$24.99**

Righteous Indignation: A Jewish Call for Justice
Edited by Rabbi Or N. Rose, Jo Ellen Green Kaiser and Margie Klein; Foreword by Rabbi David Ellenson
Leading progressive Jewish activists are gathered together in one groundbreaking volume as they explore meaningful intellectual and spiritual foundations for their social justice work.
6 x 9, 384 pp, HC, 978-1-58023-336-1 **$24.99**

Spirituality/Women's Interest

The Quotable Jewish Woman: Wisdom, Inspiration & Humor from the Mind & Heart
Edited and compiled by Elaine Bernstein Partnow
6 x 9, 496 pp, Quality PB, 978-1-58023-236-4 **$19.99**; HC, 978-1-58023-193-0 **$29.99**

The Divine Feminine in Biblical Wisdom Literature
Selections Annotated & Explained
Translated and Annotated by Rabbi Rami Shapiro
5½ x 8½, 240 pp, Quality PB, 978-1-59473-109-9 **$16.99**
(A book from SkyLight Paths, Jewish Lights' sister imprint)

The Women's Haftarah Commentary: New Insights from Women Rabbis on the 54 Weekly Haftarah Portions, the 5 Megillot & Special Shabbatot
Edited by Rabbi Elyse Goldstein
In this groundbreaking book, more than fifty women rabbis come together to offer us inspiring insights on the Torah, in a week-by-week format.
6 x 9, 560 pp, Quality PB, 978-1-58023-371-2 **$19.99**; HC, 978-1-58023-133-6 **$39.99**

The Women's Torah Commentary: New Insights from Women Rabbis on the 54 Weekly Torah Portions
Edited by Rabbi Elyse Goldstein
This compendium will challenge—and possibly change—the way you experience Judaism as it illuminates the historical significance of female portrayals in the Haftarah and the Five Megillot.
6 x 9, 496 pp, Quality PB, 978-1-58023-370-5 **$19.99**; HC, 978-1-58023-076-6 **$34.95**

The Year Mom Got Religion: One Woman's Midlife Journey into Judaism
By Lee Meyerhoff Hendler
6 x 9, 208 pp, Quality PB, 978-1-58023-070-4 **$15.95**

> See Holidays for *The Women's Passover Companion: Women's Reflections on the Festival of Freedom* and *The Women's Seder Sourcebook: Rituals & Readings for Use at the Passover Seder.*

Inspiration

Happiness and the Human Spirit: The Spirituality of Becoming the Best You Can Be *By Abraham J. Twerski, MD*
Shows you that true happiness is attainable once you stop looking outside yourself for the source.
6 x 9, 176 pp, Quality PB, 978-1-58023-404-7 **$16.99**; HC, 978-1-58023-343-9 **$19.99**

Life's Daily Blessings: Inspiring Reflections on Gratitude and Joy for Every Day, Based on Jewish Wisdom *By Rabbi Kerry M. Olitzky* 4½ x 6½, 368 pp, Quality PB, 978-1-58023-396-5 **$16.99**

The Bridge to Forgiveness: Stories and Prayers for Finding God and Restoring Wholeness *By Rabbi Karyn D. Kedar*
Examines how forgiveness can be the bridge that connects us to wholeness and peace.
6 x 9, 176 pp, HC, 978-1-58023-324-8 **$19.99**

God's To-Do List: 103 Ways to Be an Angel and Do God's Work on Earth
By Dr. Ron Wolfson 6 x 9, 150 pp, Quality PB, 978-1-58023-301-9 **$16.99**

God in All Moments: Mystical & Practical Spiritual Wisdom from Hasidic Masters
Edited and translated by Or N. Rose with Ebn D. Leader
5½ x 8½, 192 pp, Quality PB, 978-1-58023-186-2 **$16.95**

Our Dance with God: Finding Prayer, Perspective and Meaning in the Stories of Our Lives *By Karyn D. Kedar* 6 x 9, 176 pp, Quality PB, 978-1-58023-202-9 **$16.99**

Also Available: **The Dance of the Dolphin** (HC edition of Our Dance with God)
6 x 9, 176 pp, HC, 978-1-58023-202-9 **$19.95**

The Empty Chair: Finding Hope and Joy—Timeless Wisdom from a Hasidic Master, Rebbe Nachman of Breslov *Adapted by Moshe Mykoff and the Breslov Research Institute*
4 x 6, 128 pp, 2-color text, Deluxe PB w/flaps, 978-1-879045-67-5 **$9.99**

The Gentle Weapon: Prayers for Everyday and Not-So-Everyday Moments—Timeless Wisdom from the Teachings of the Hasidic Master, Rebbe Nachman of Breslov *Adapted by Moshe Mykoff and S. C. Mizrahi, together with the Breslov Research Institute*
4 x 6, 144 pp, 2-color text, Deluxe PB w/flaps, 978-1-58023-022-3 **$9.99**

God Whispers: Stories of the Soul, Lessons of the Heart *By Karyn D. Kedar*
6 x 9, 176 pp, Quality PB, 978-1-58023-088-9 **$15.95**

Restful Reflections: Nighttime Inspiration to Calm the Soul, Based on Jewish Wisdom
By Rabbi Kerry M. Olitzky & Rabbi Lori Forman 4½ x 6½, 448 pp, Quality PB, 978-1-58023-091-9 **$15.95**

Sacred Intentions: Daily Inspiration to Strengthen the Spirit, Based on Jewish Wisdom
By Rabbi Kerry M. Olitzky and Rabbi Lori Forman 4½ x 6½, 448 pp, Quality PB, 978-1-58023-061-2 **$15.95**

Kabbalah/Mysticism

Seek My Face: A Jewish Mystical Theology *By Arthur Green*
6 x 9, 304 pp, Quality PB, 978-1-58023-130-5 **$19.95**

Zohar: Annotated & Explained *Translation and annotation by Daniel C. Matt; Foreword by Andrew Harvey* 5½ x 8½, 176 pp, Quality PB, 978-1-893361-51-5 **$15.99**
(A book from SkyLight Paths, Jewish Lights' sister imprint)

Ehyeh: A Kabbalah for Tomorrow
By Arthur Green 6 x 9, 224 pp, Quality PB, 978-1-58023-213-5 **$16.99**

The Flame of the Heart: Prayers of a Chasidic Mystic *By Reb Noson of Breslov. Translated by David Sears with the Breslov Research Institute* 5 x 7¼, 160 pp, Quality PB, 978-1-58023-246-3 **$15.99**

The Gift of Kabbalah: Discovering the Secrets of Heaven, Renewing Your Life on Earth
By Tamar Frankiel, PhD 6 x 9, 256 pp, Quality PB, 978-1-58023-141-1 **$16.95**
HC, 978-1-58023-108-4 **$21.95**

Kabbalah: A Brief Introduction for Christians
By Tamar Frankiel, PhD 5½ x 8½, 208 pp, Quality PB, 978-1-58023-303-3 **$16.99**

The Lost Princess and Other Kabbalistic Tales of Rebbe Nachman of Breslov
The Seven Beggars and Other Kabbalistic Tales of Rebbe Nachman of Breslov
Translated by Rabbi Aryeh Kaplan; Preface by Rabbi Chaim Kramer
Lost Princess: 6 x 9, 400 pp, Quality PB, 978-1-58023-217-3 **$18.99**
Seven Beggars: 6 x 9, 192 pp, Quality PB, 978-1-58023-250-0 **$16.99**

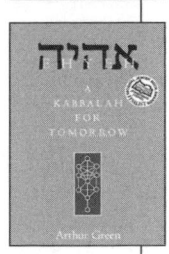

See also *The Way Into Jewish Mystical Tradition* in Spirituality / The Way Into... Series

About Jewish Lights

People of all faiths and backgrounds yearn for books that attract, engage, educate, and spiritually inspire.

Our principal goal is to stimulate thought and help all people learn about who the Jewish People are, where they come from, and what the future can be made to hold. While people of our diverse Jewish heritage are the primary audience, our books speak to people in the Christian world as well and will broaden their understanding of Judaism and the roots of their own faith.

We bring to you authors who are at the forefront of spiritual thought and experience. While each has something different to say, they all say it in a voice that you can hear.

Our books are designed to welcome you and then to engage, stimulate, and inspire. We judge our success not only by whether or not our books are beautiful and commercially successful, but by whether or not they make a difference in your life.

For your information and convenience, at the back of this book we have provided a list of other Jewish Lights books you might find interesting and useful. They cover all the categories of your life:

Bar/Bat Mitzvah
Bible Study / Midrash
Children's Books
Congregation Resources
Current Events / History
Ecology / Environment
Fiction: Mystery, Science Fiction
Grief / Healing
Holidays / Holy Days
Inspiration
Kabbalah / Mysticism / Enneagram

Life Cycle
Meditation
Parenting
Prayer
Ritual / Sacred Practice
Spirituality
Theology / Philosophy
Travel
12-Step
Women's Interest

Stuart M. Matlins, Publisher

Or phone, fax, mail or e-mail to: **JEWISH LIGHTS Publishing**
Sunset Farm Offices, Route 4 • P.O. Box 237 • Woodstock, Vermont 05091
Tel: (802) 457-4000 • Fax: (802) 457-4004 • www.jewishlights.com
Credit card orders: **(800) 962-4544** (8:30AM–5:30PM ET Monday–Friday)
Generous discounts on quantity orders. SATISFACTION GUARANTEED. Prices subject to change.

For more information about each book, visit our website at www.jewishlights.com